"That love is inexhaustible, you will be there"

forever

THIS BOOK

Belongs to

Visit Our Author Page At

amazon.com

Scan me

TURKEY COLORING BOOK

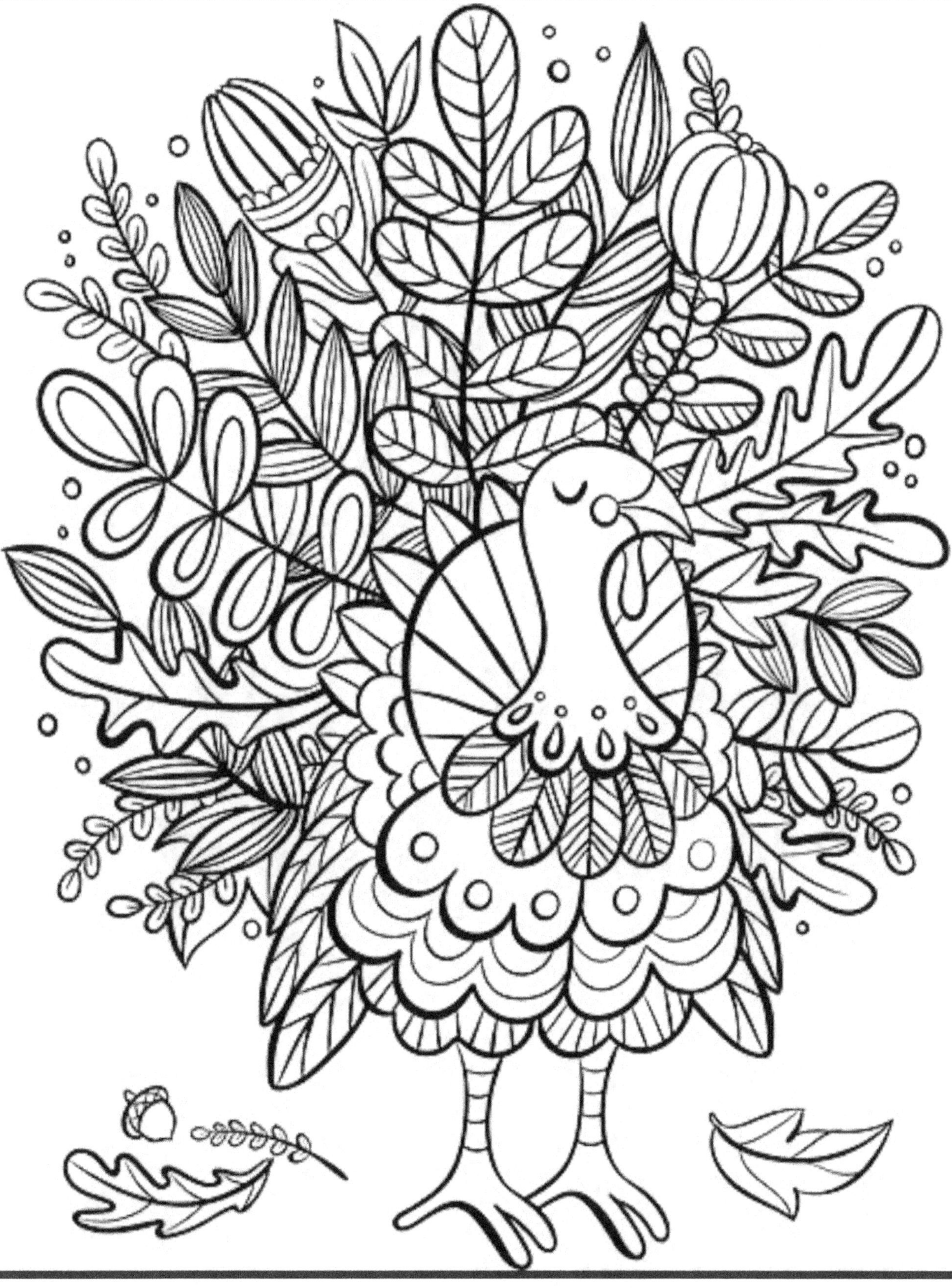

TURKEY COLORING BOOK

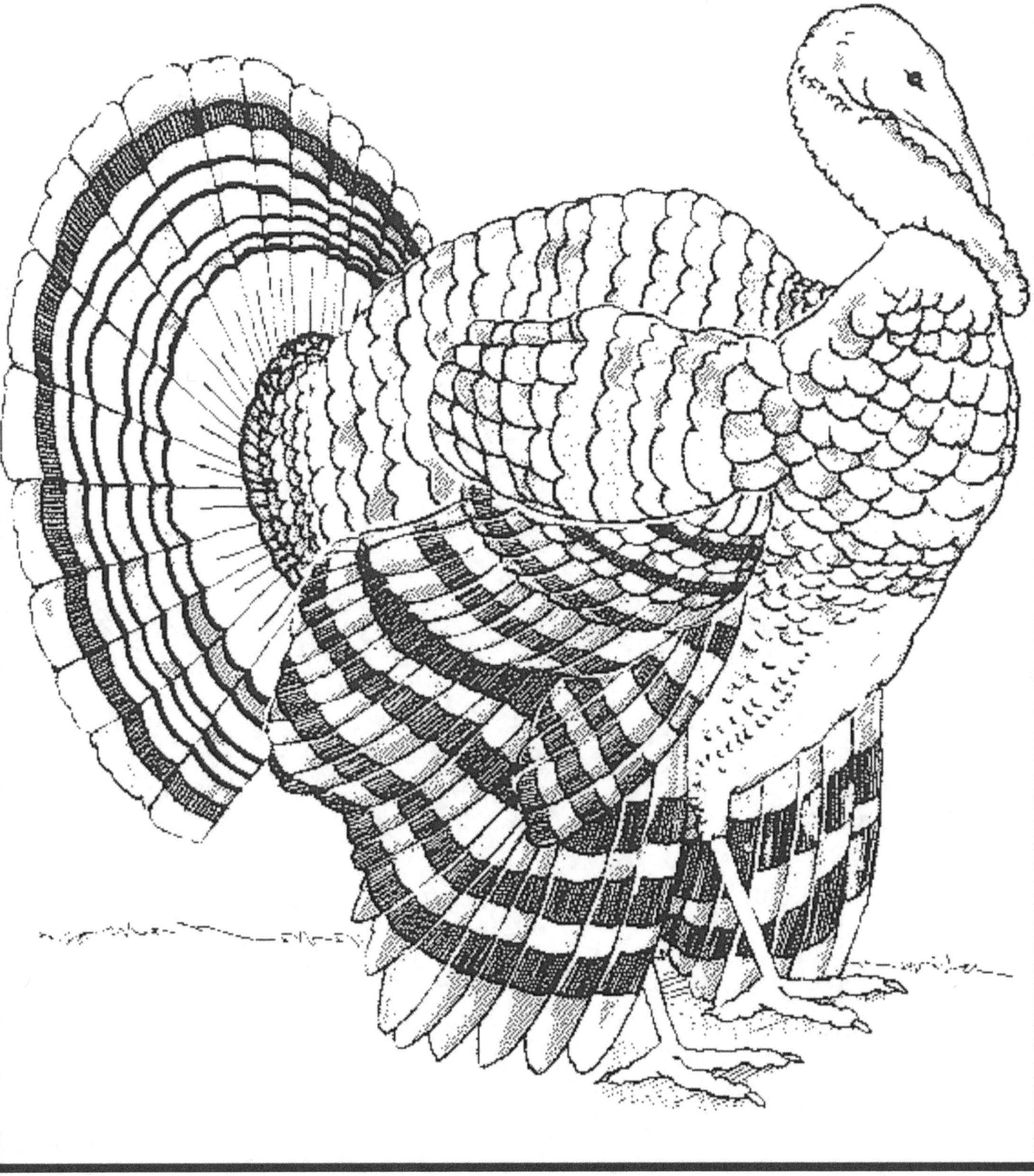

TURKEY COLORING BOOK

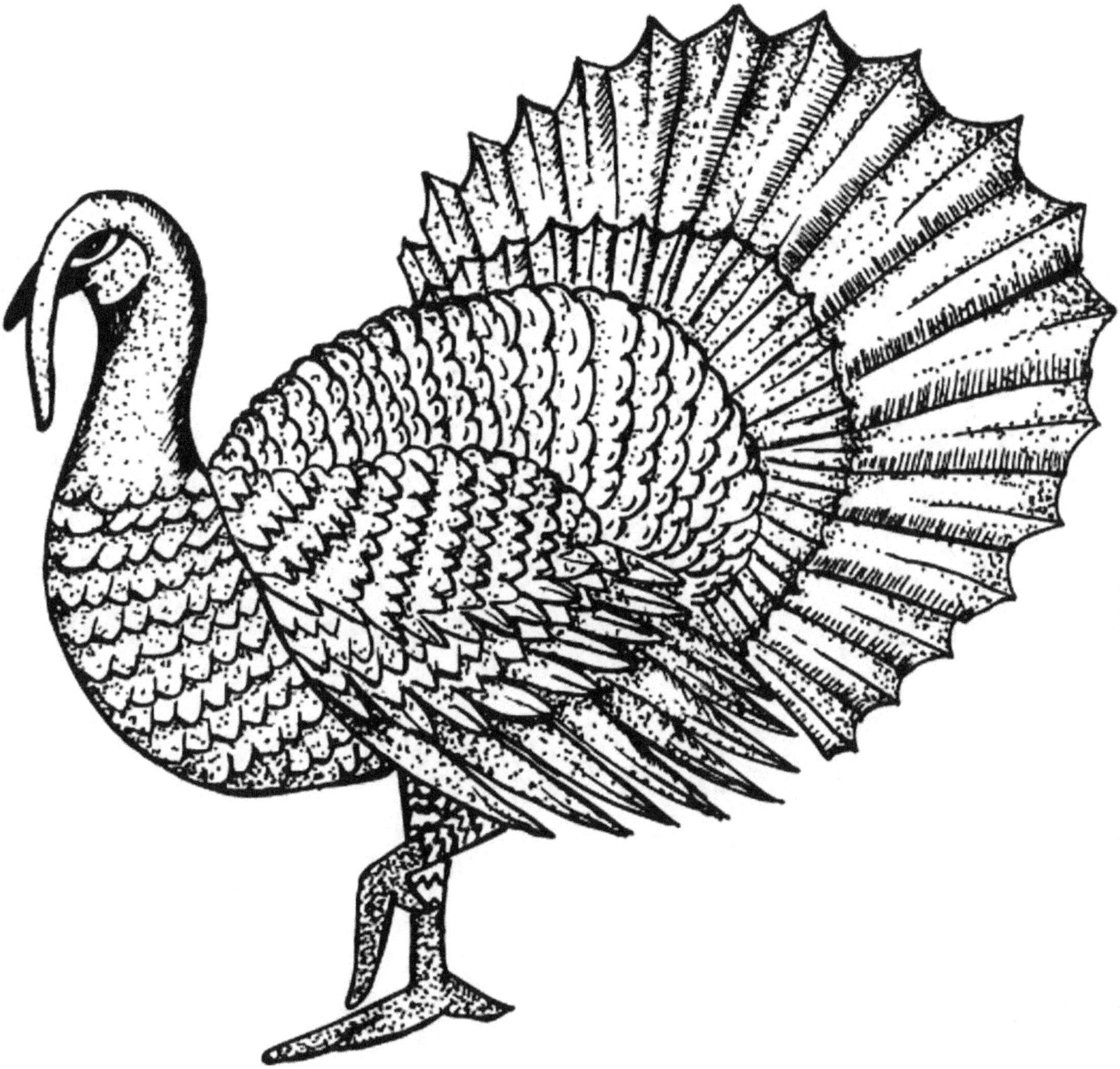

TURKEY COLORING BOOK

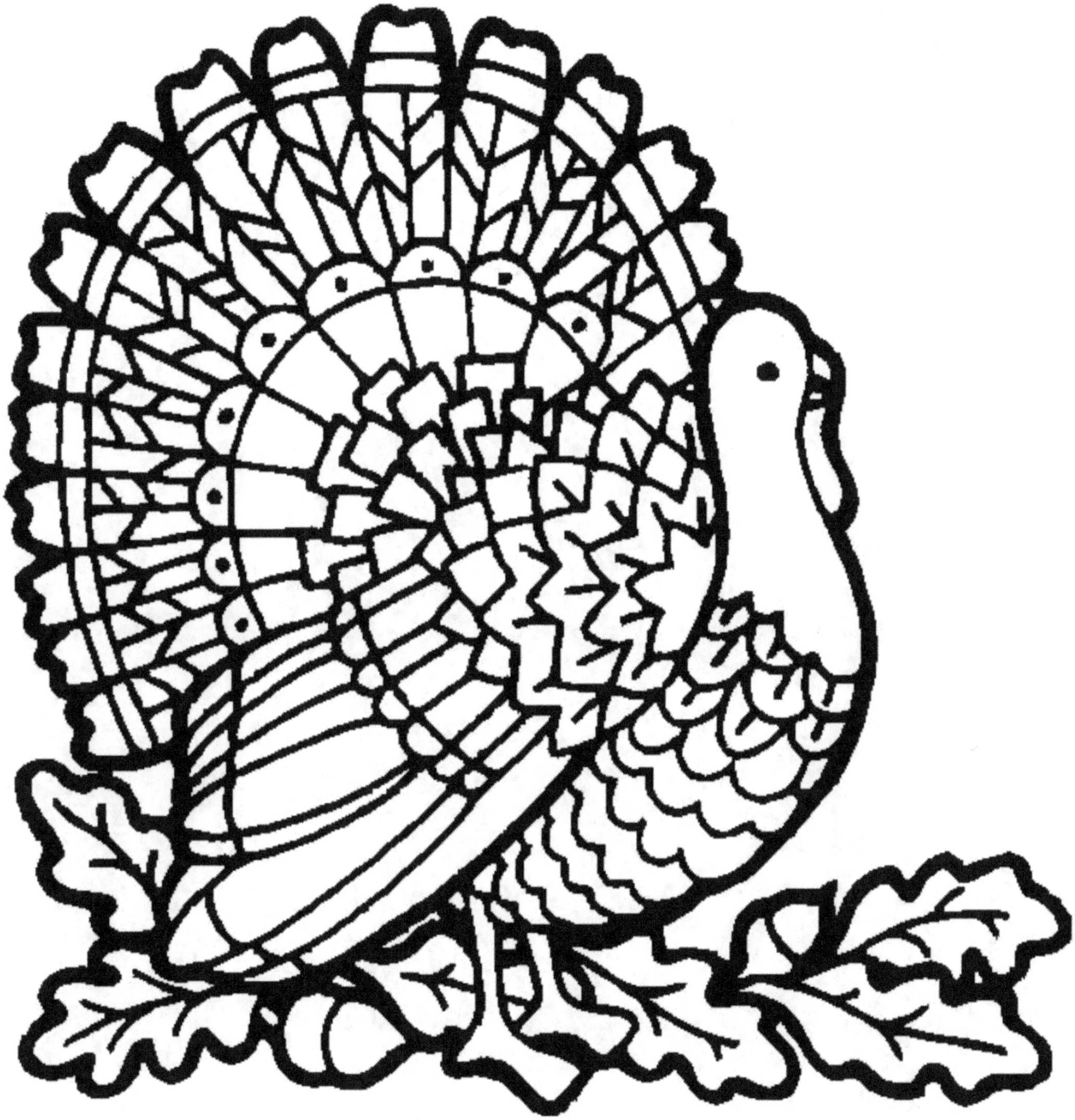

TURKEY COLORING BOOK

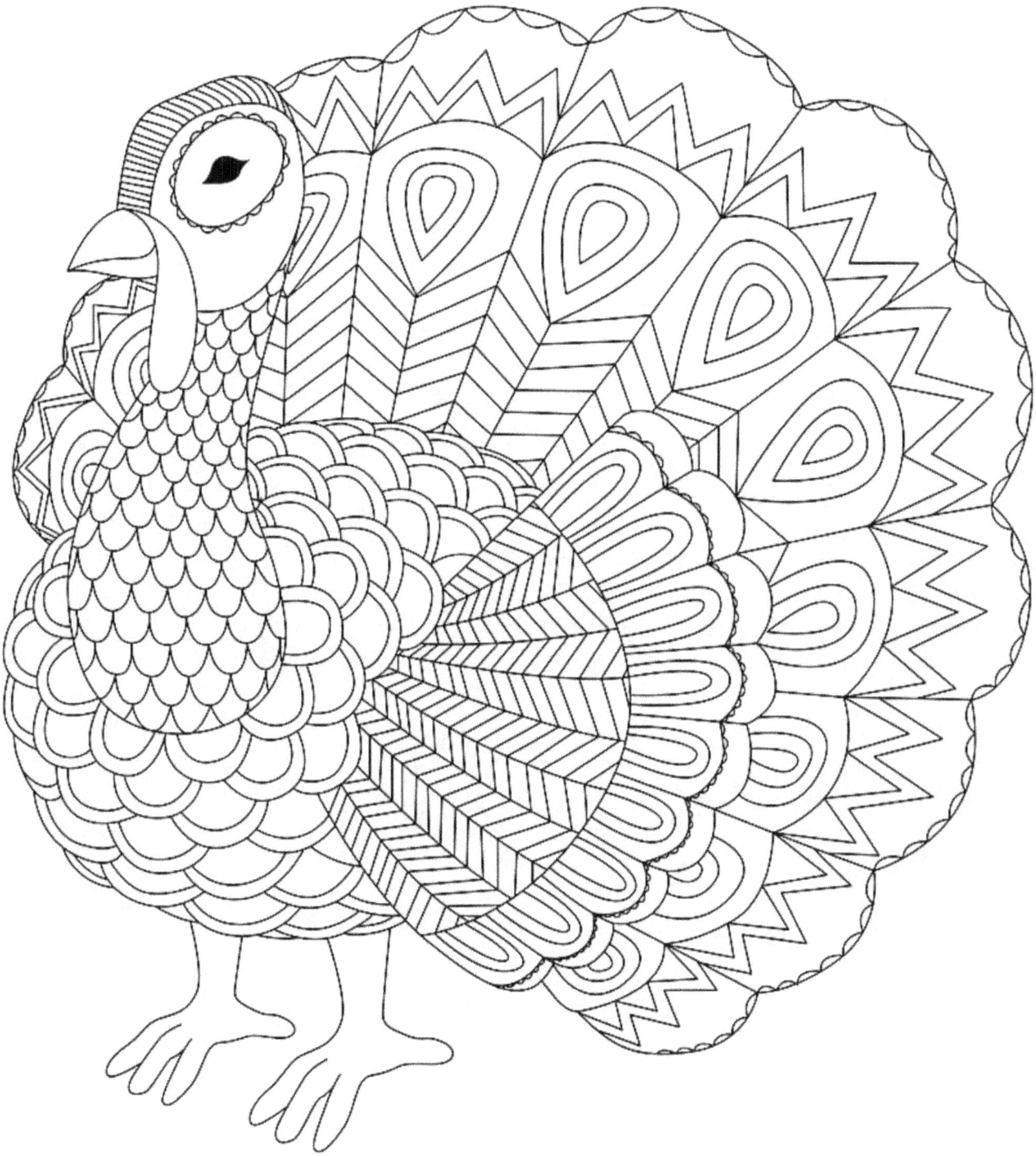

TURKEY COLORING BOOK

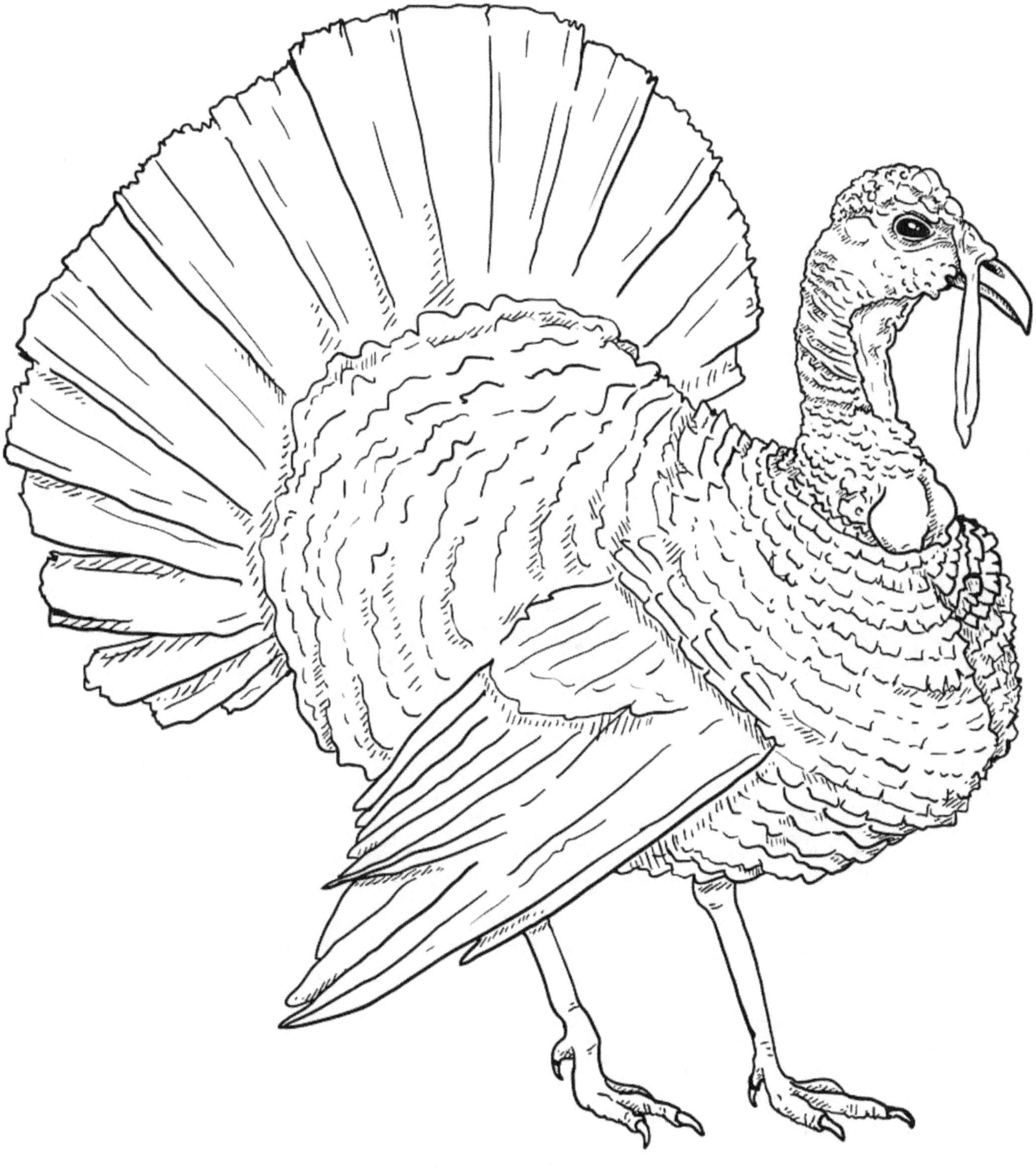

TURKEY COLORING BOOK

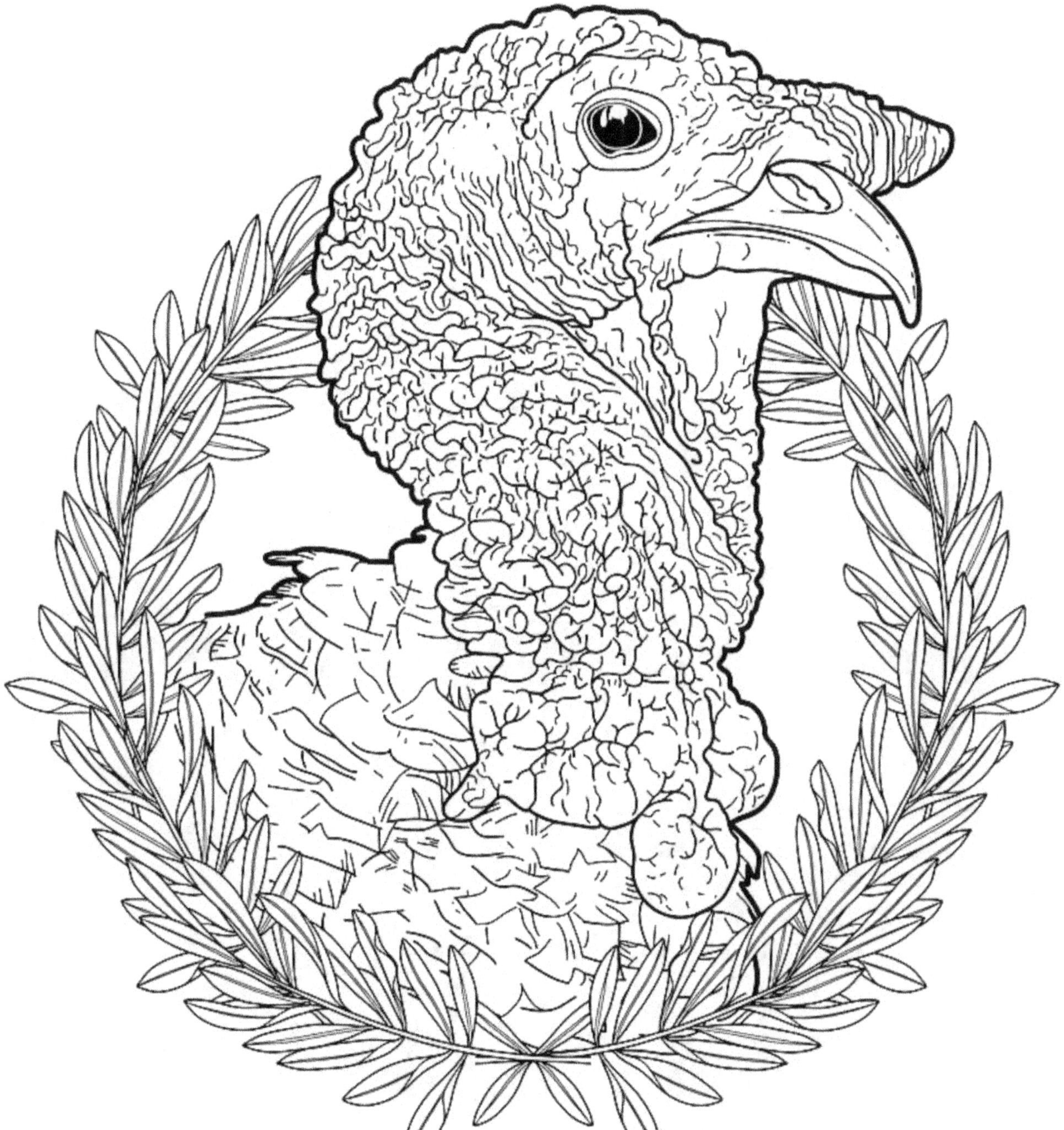

TURKEY COLORING BOOK

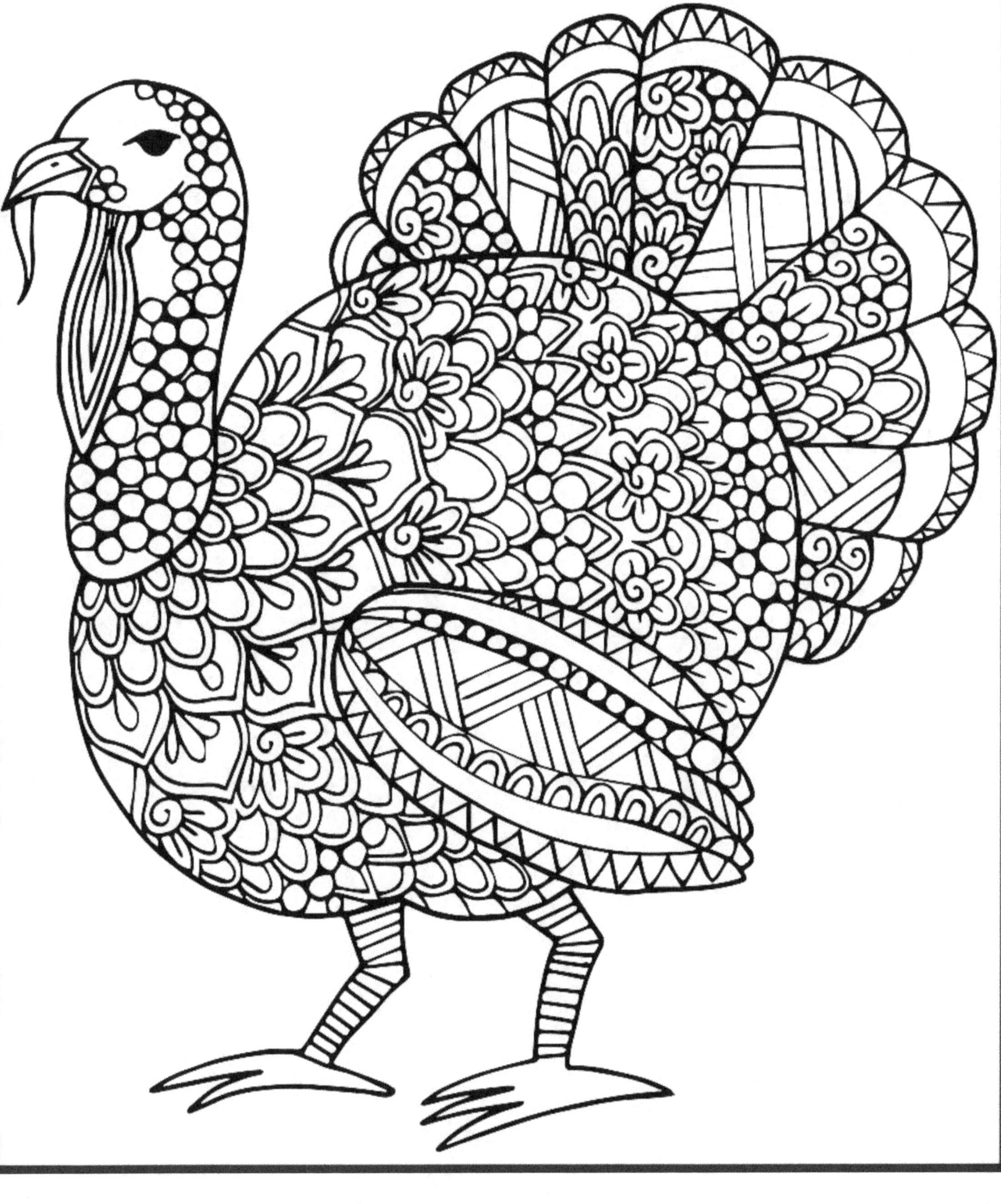

TURKEY COLORING BOOK

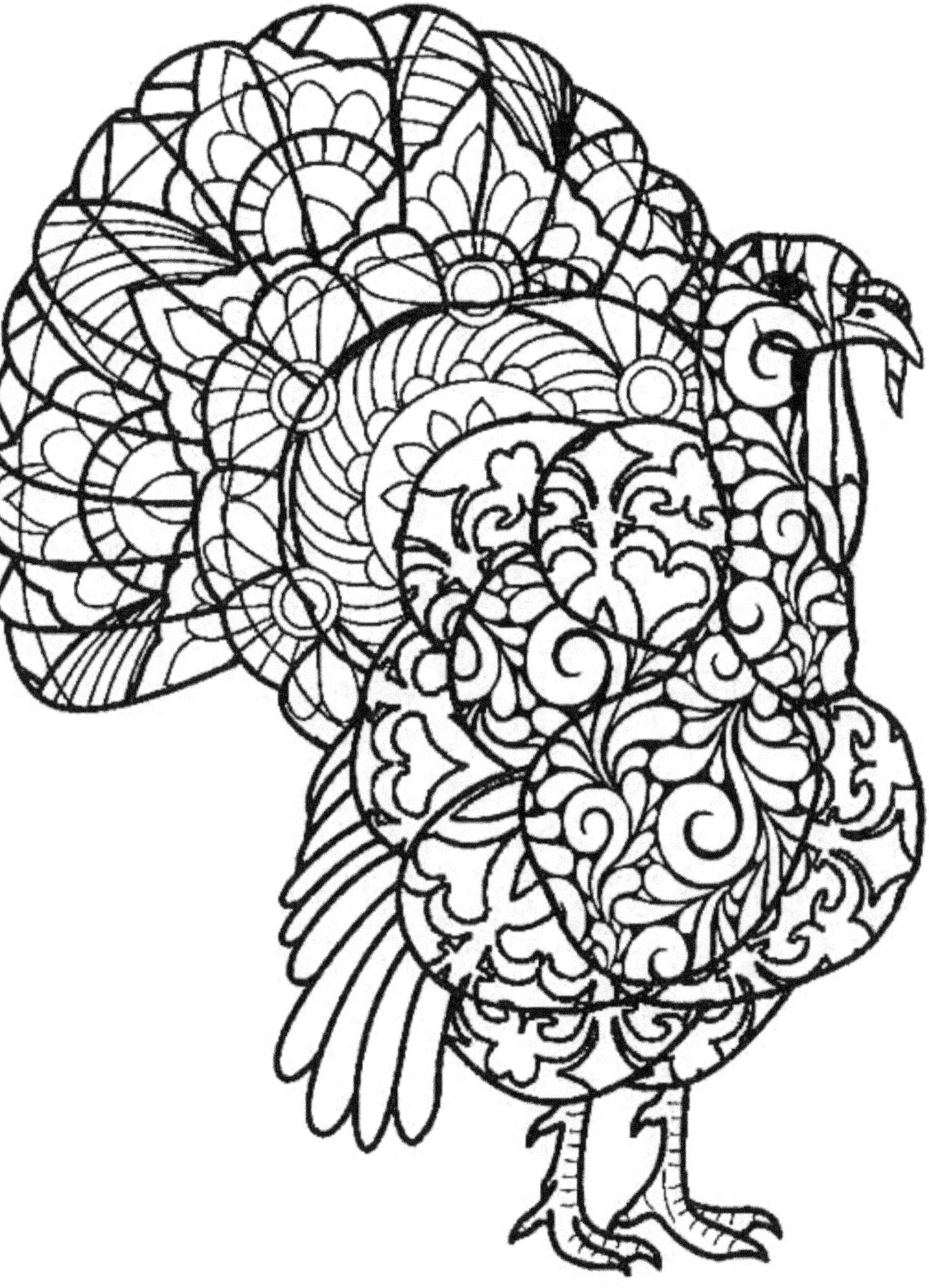

TURKEY COLORING BOOK

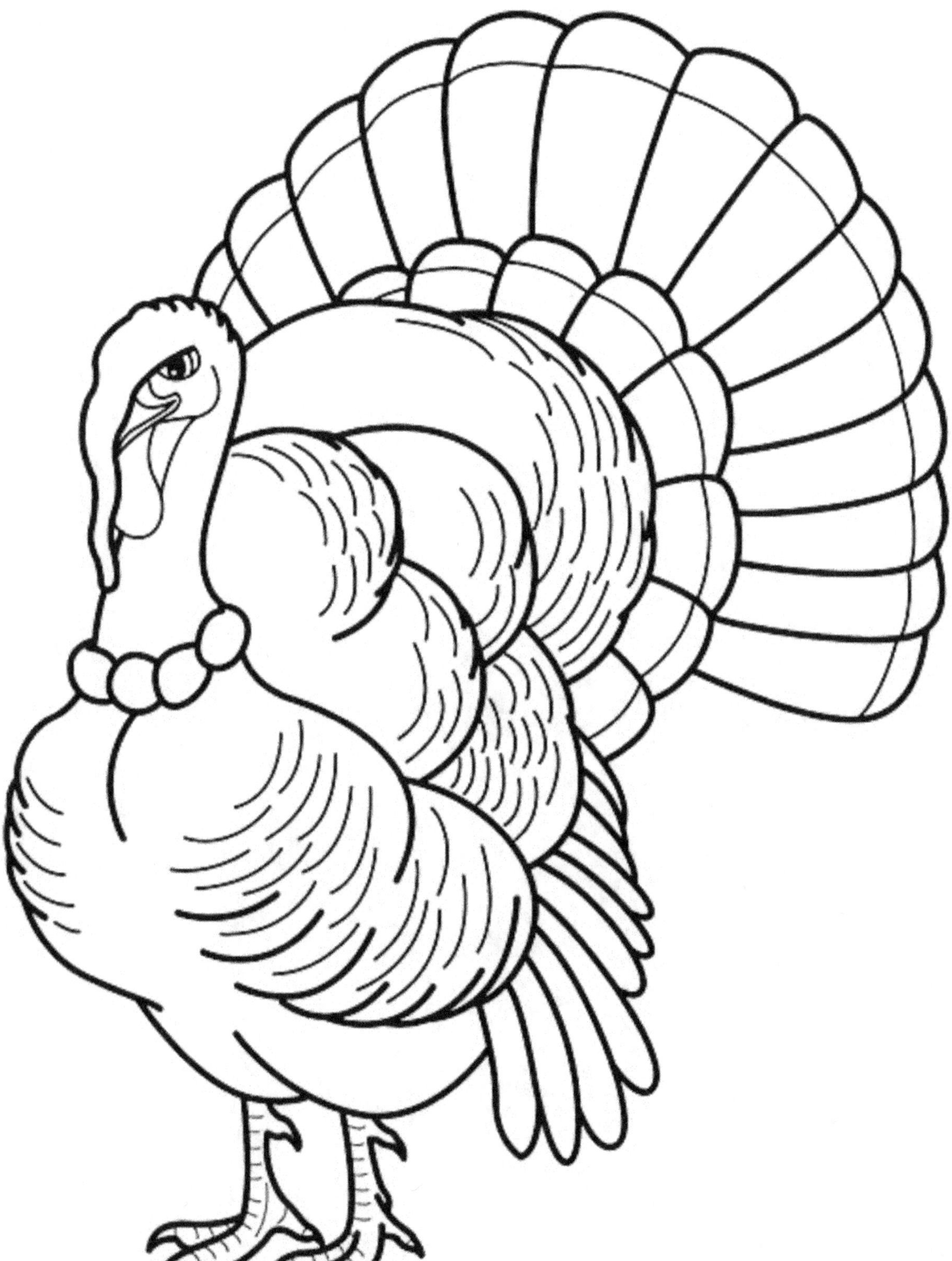

TURKEY COLORING BOOK

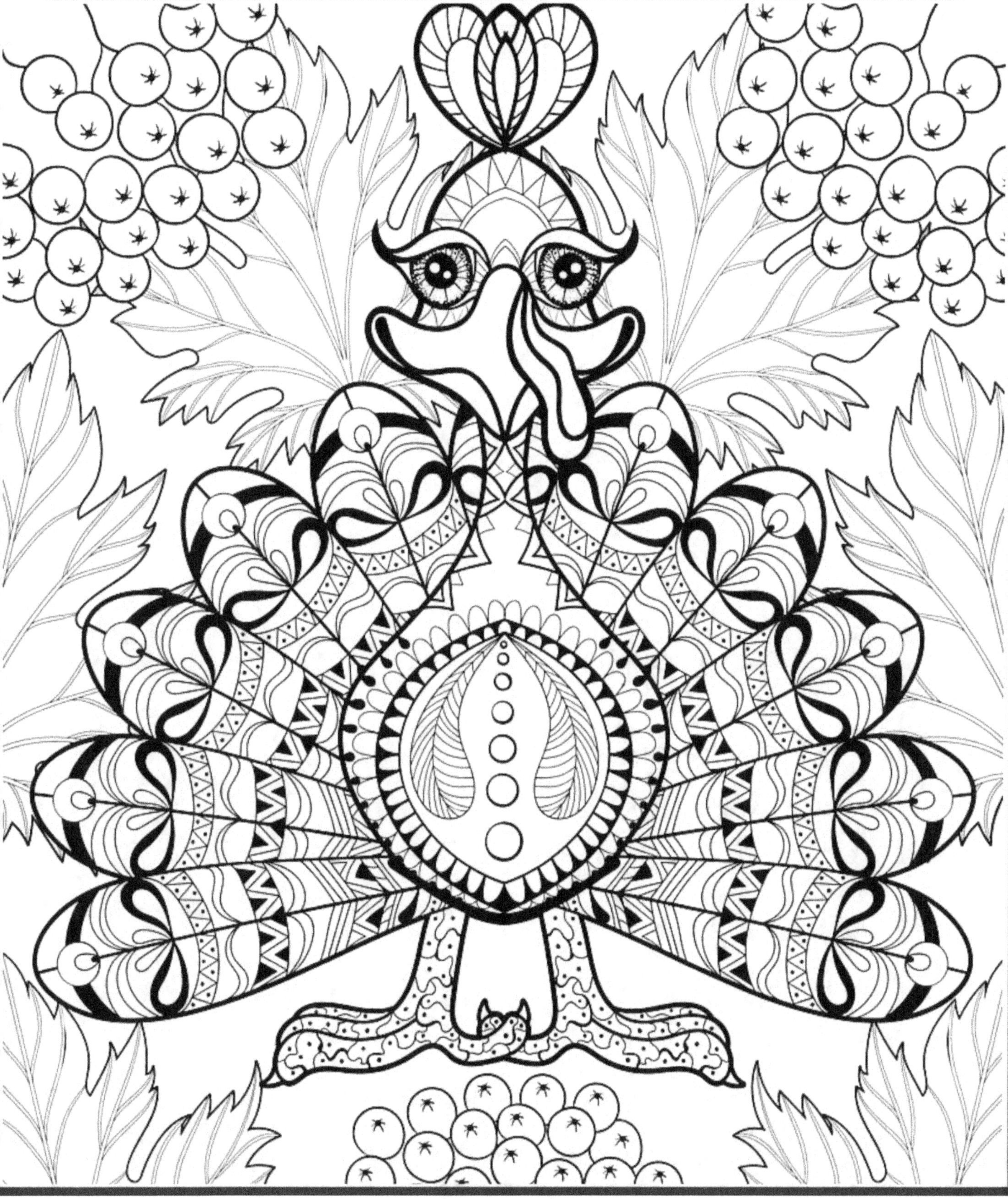

TURKEY COLORING BOOK

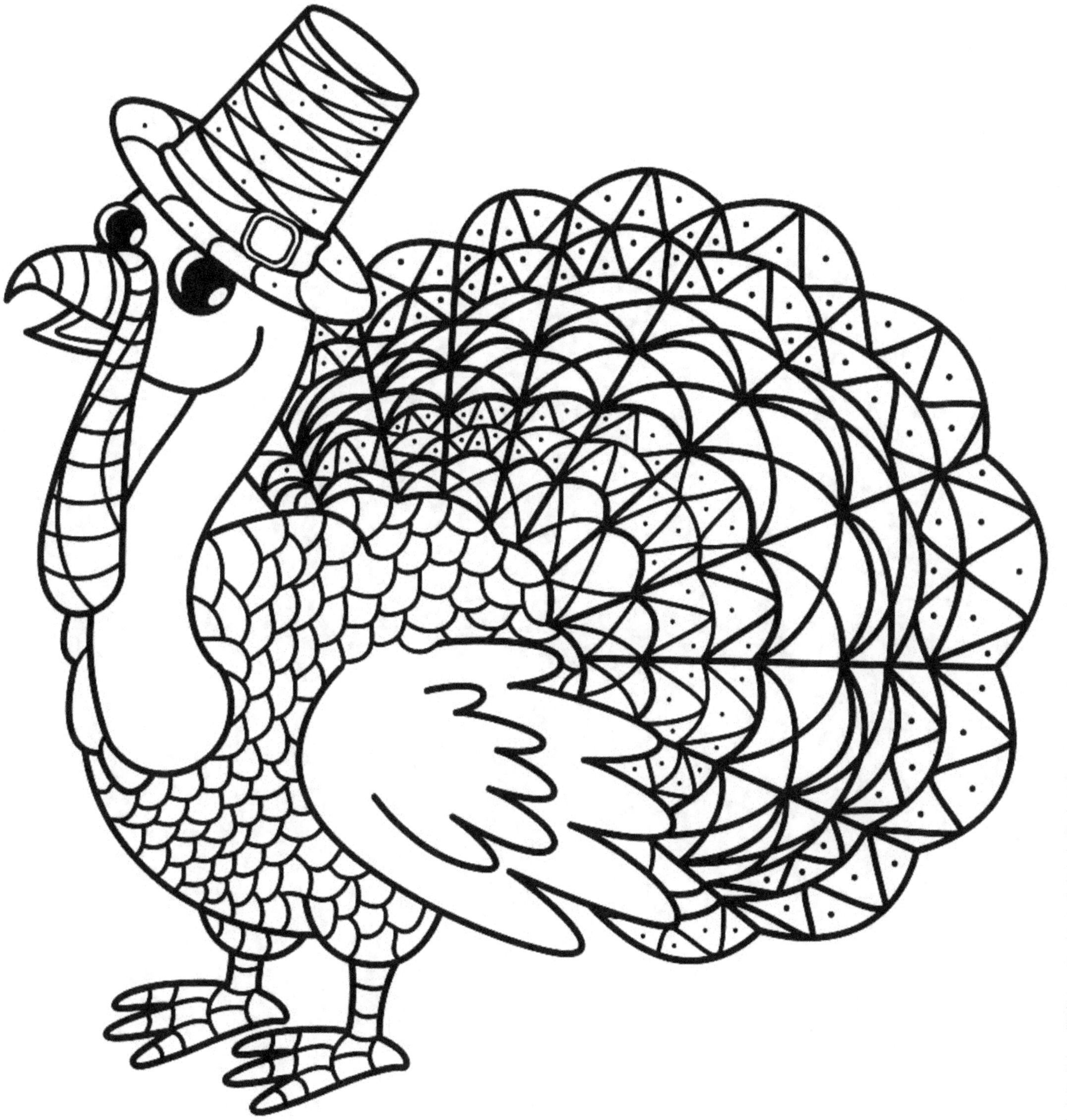

TURKEY COLORING BOOK

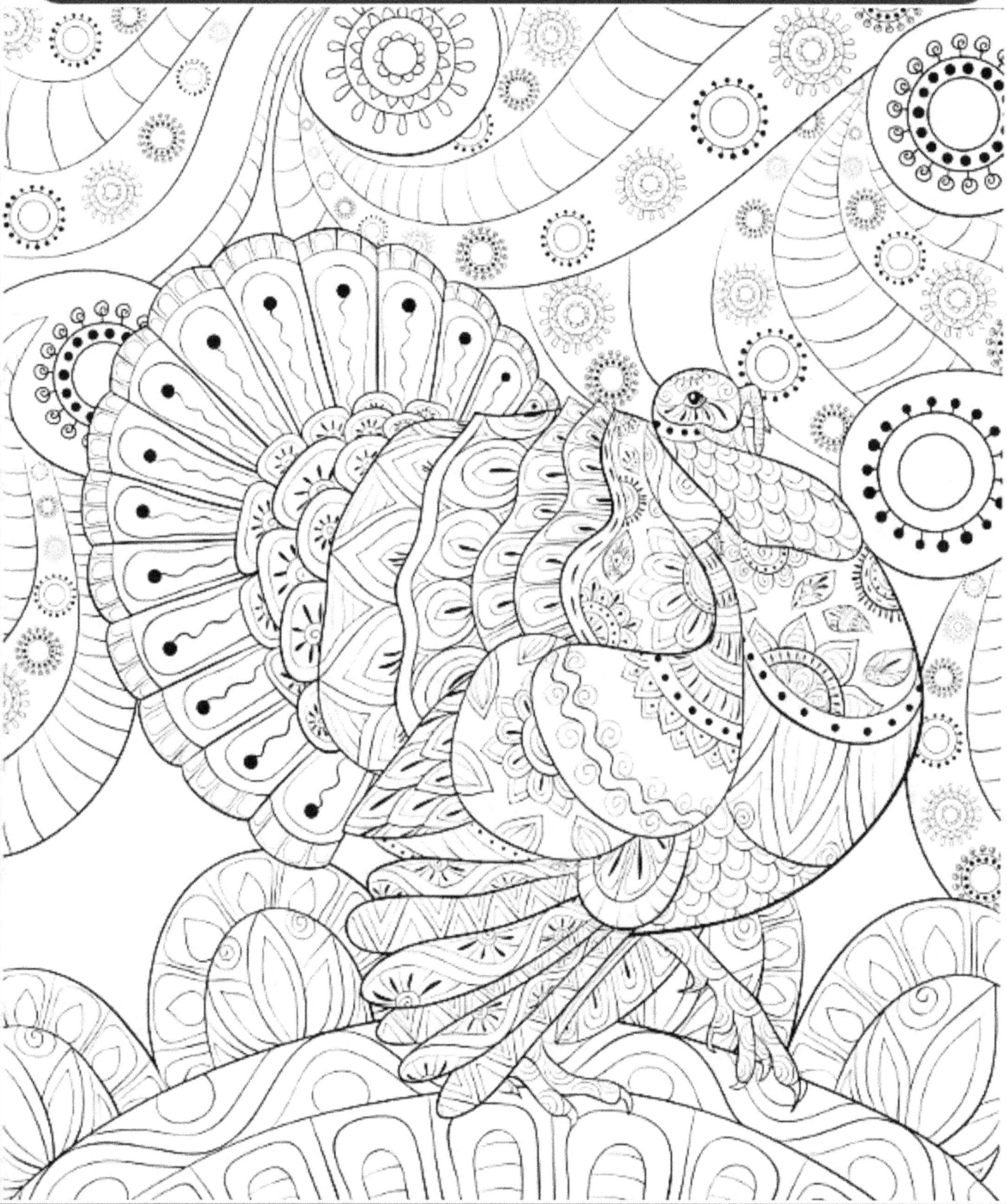

TURKEY COLORING BOOK

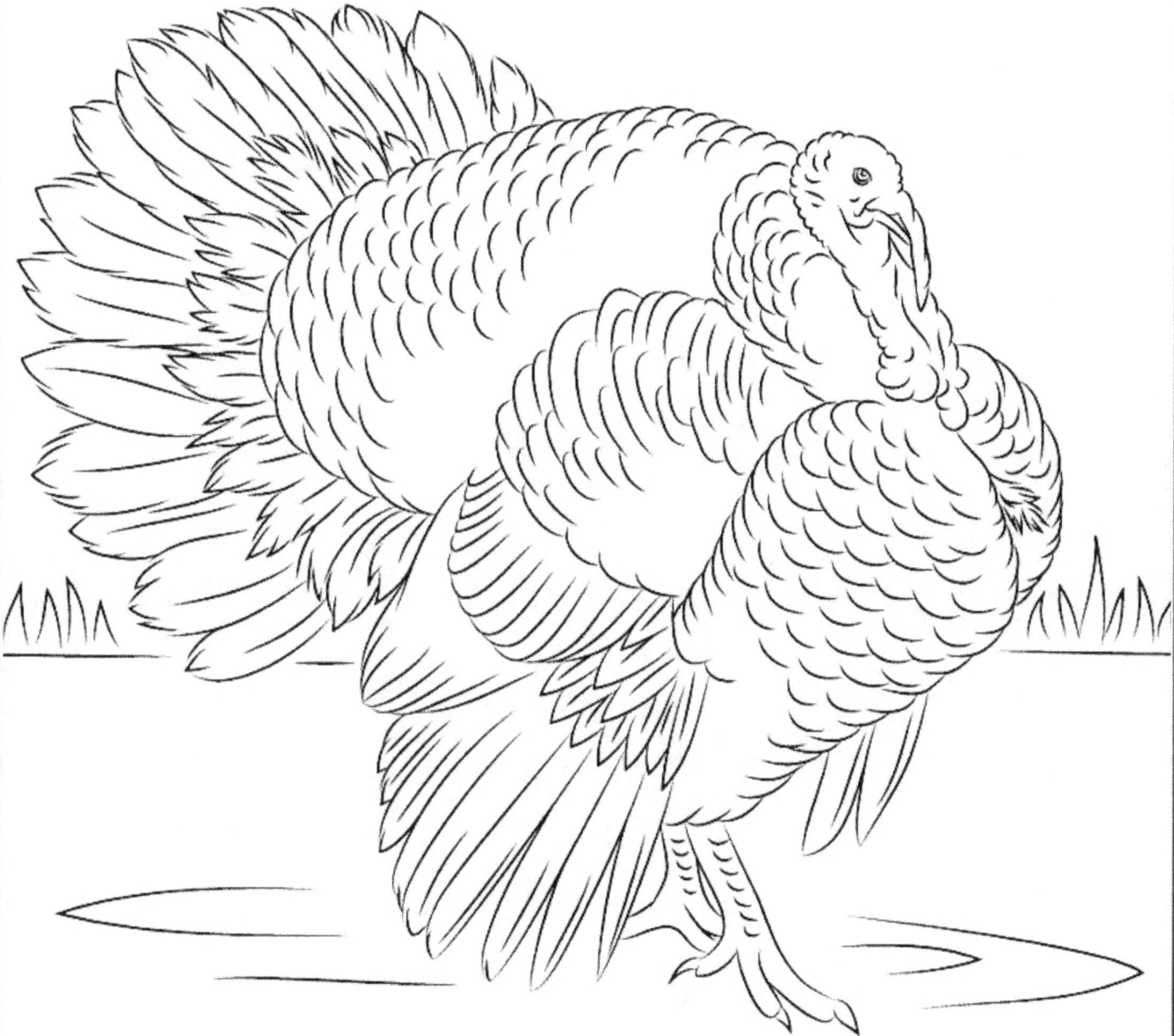

TURKEY COLORING BOOK

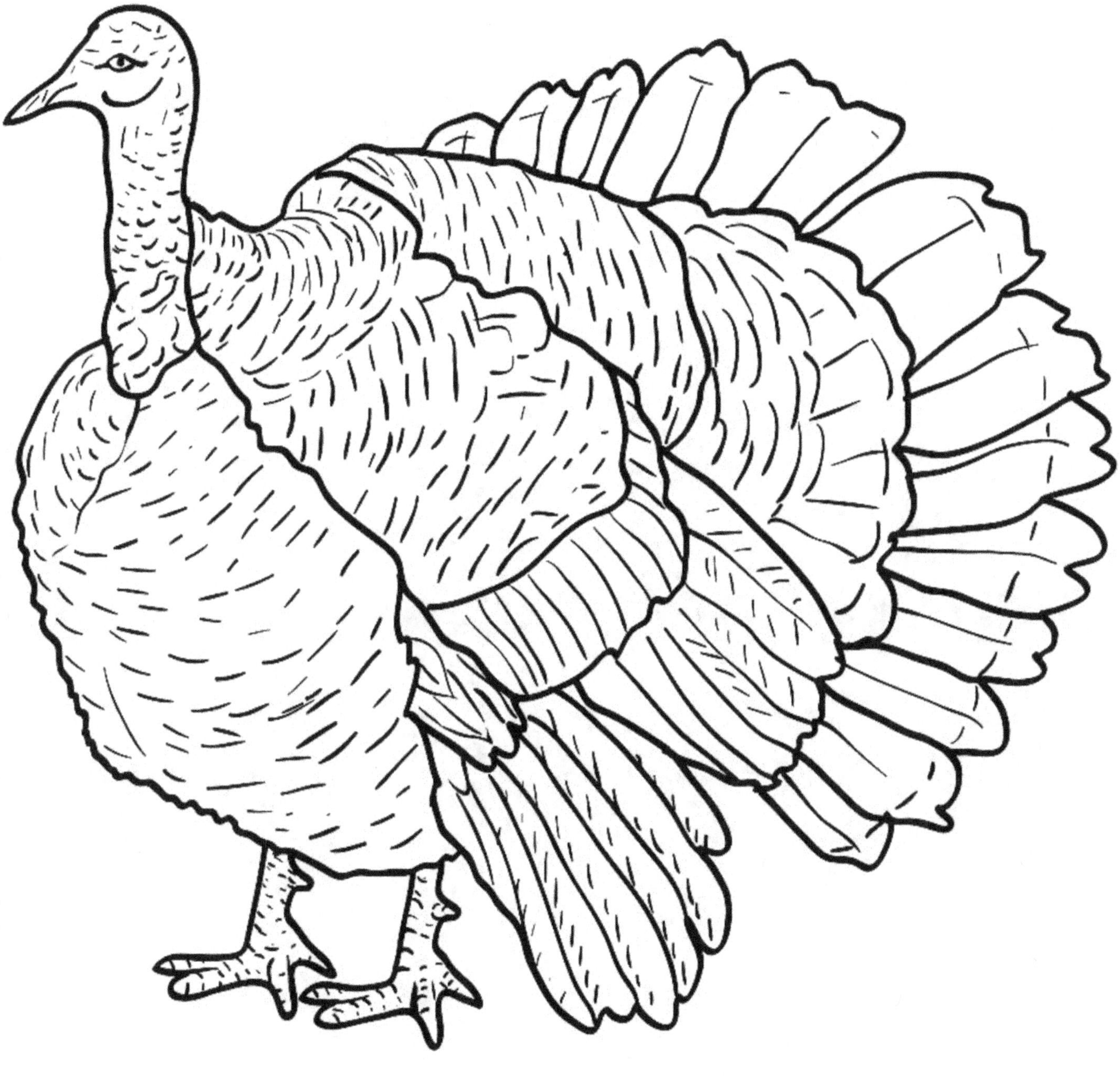

TURKEY COLORING BOOK

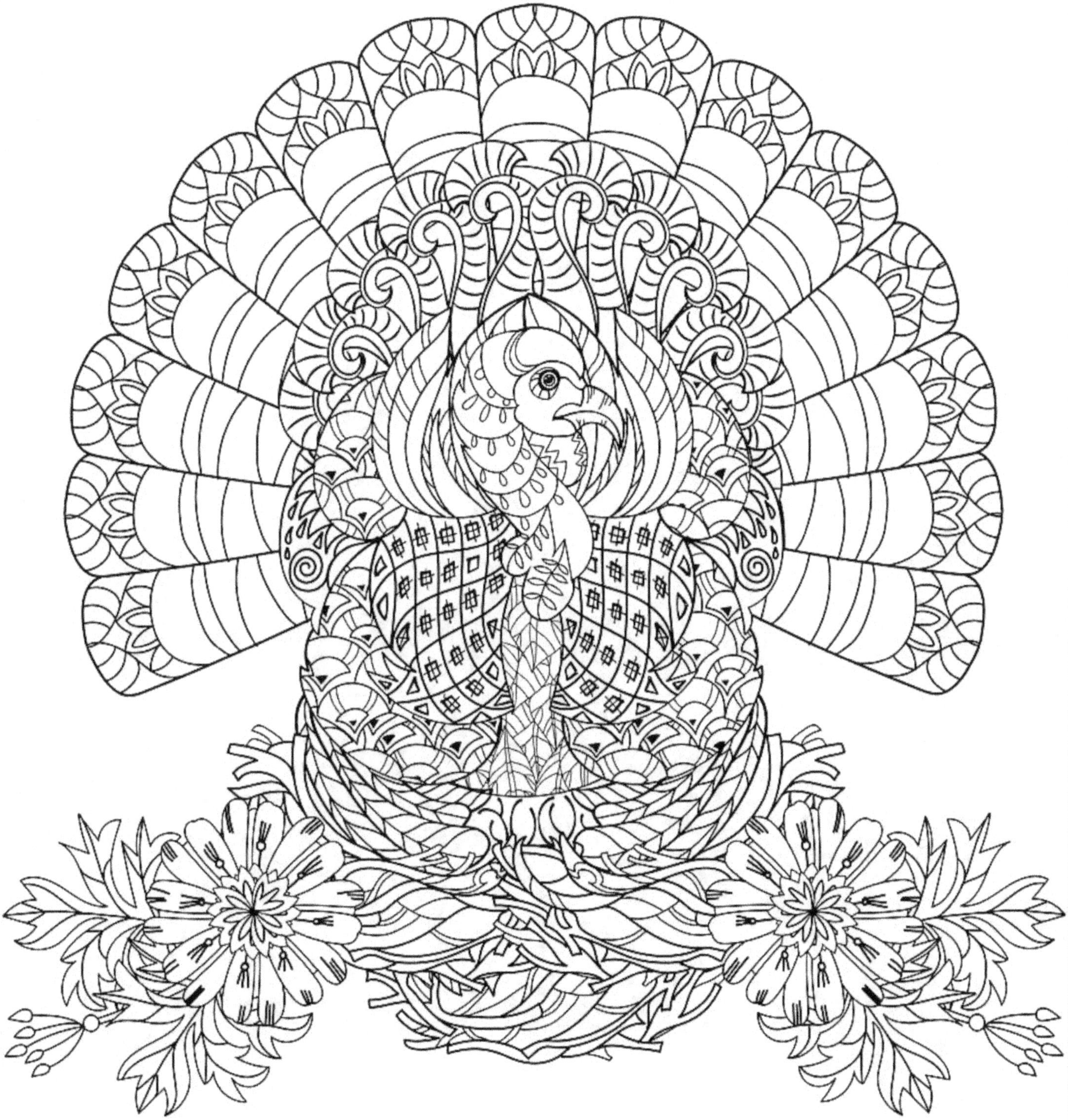

TURKEY COLORING BOOK

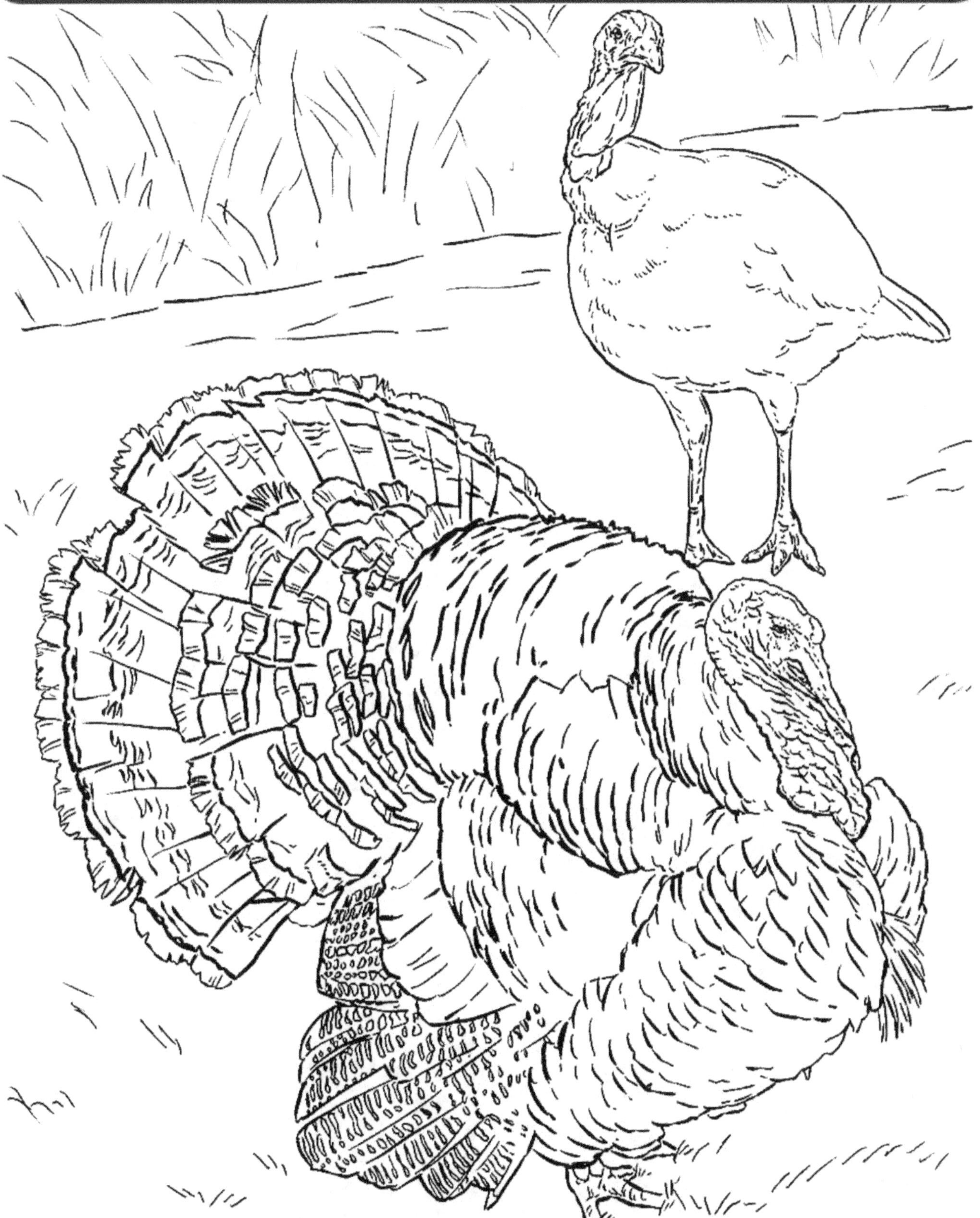

TURKEY COLORING BOOK

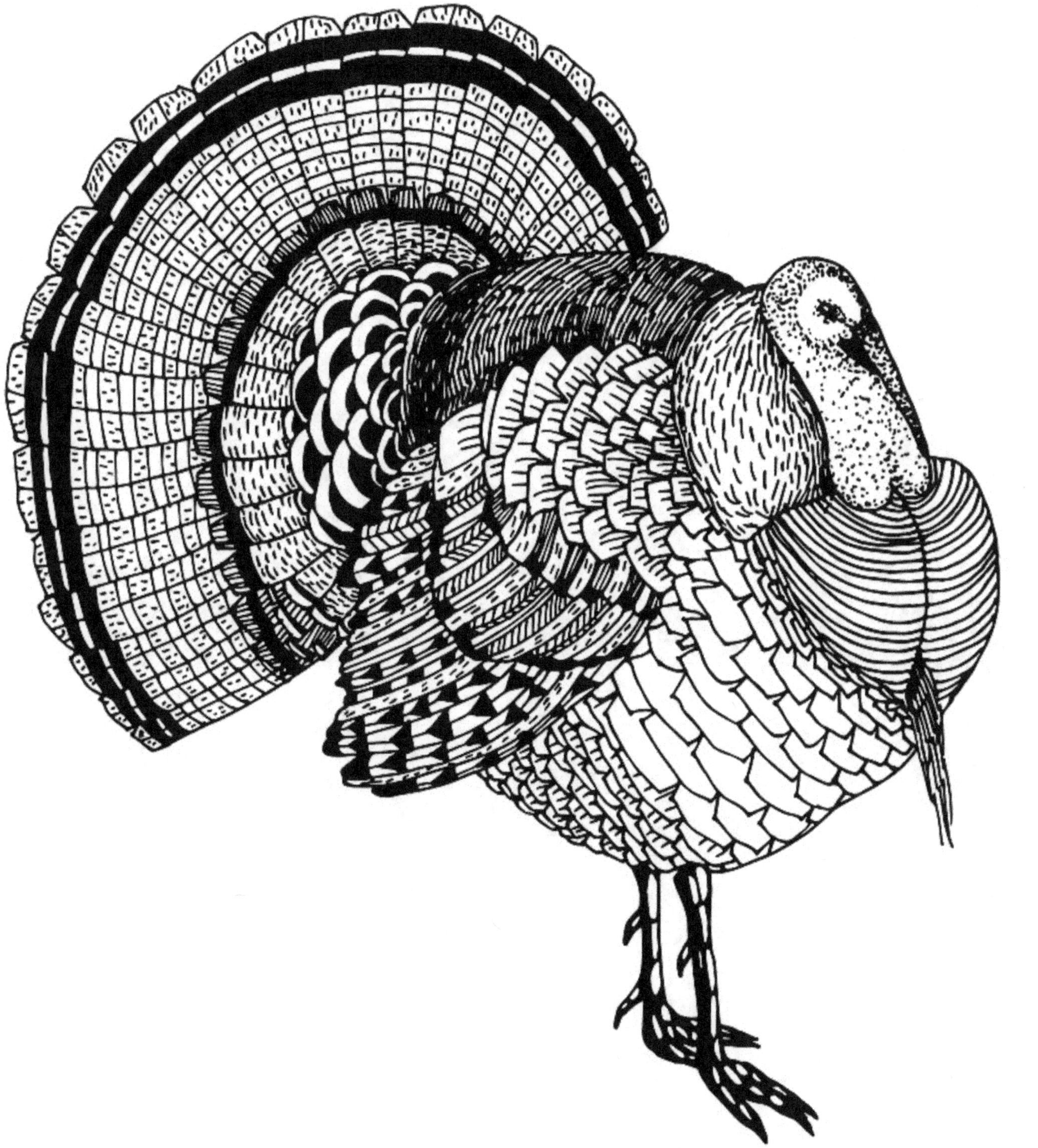

TURKEY COLORING BOOK

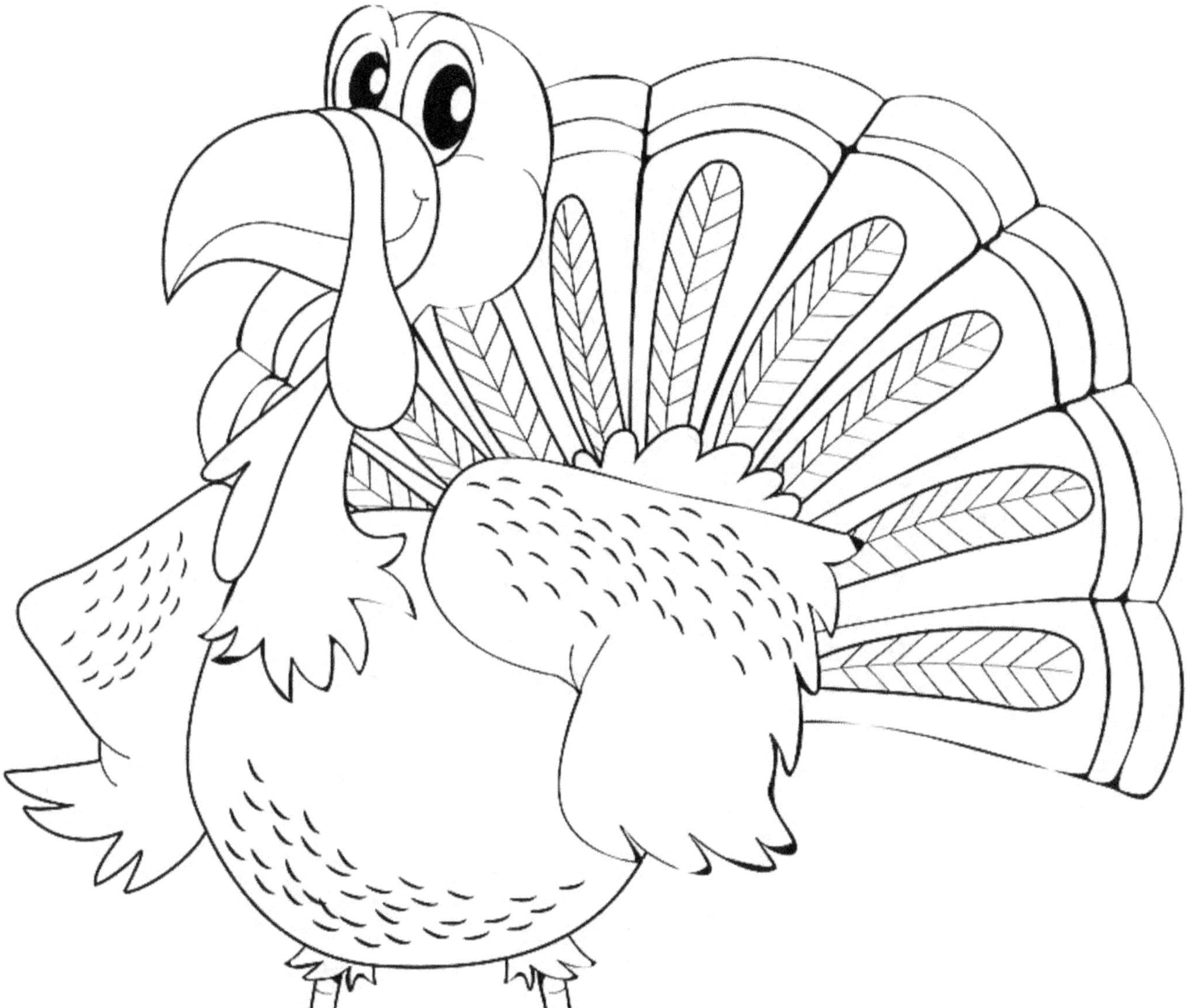

TURKEY COLORING BOOK

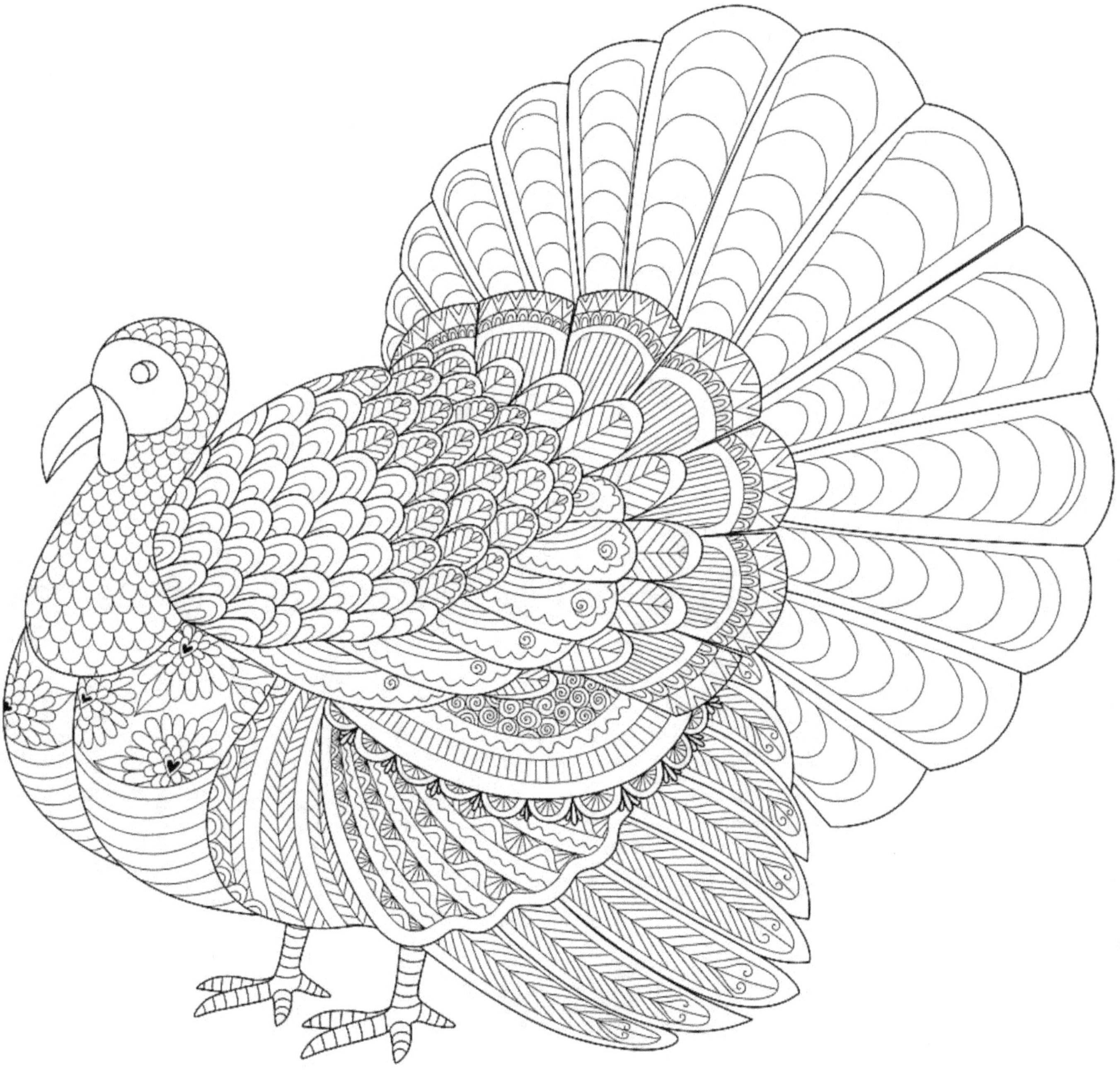

TURKEY COLORING BOOK

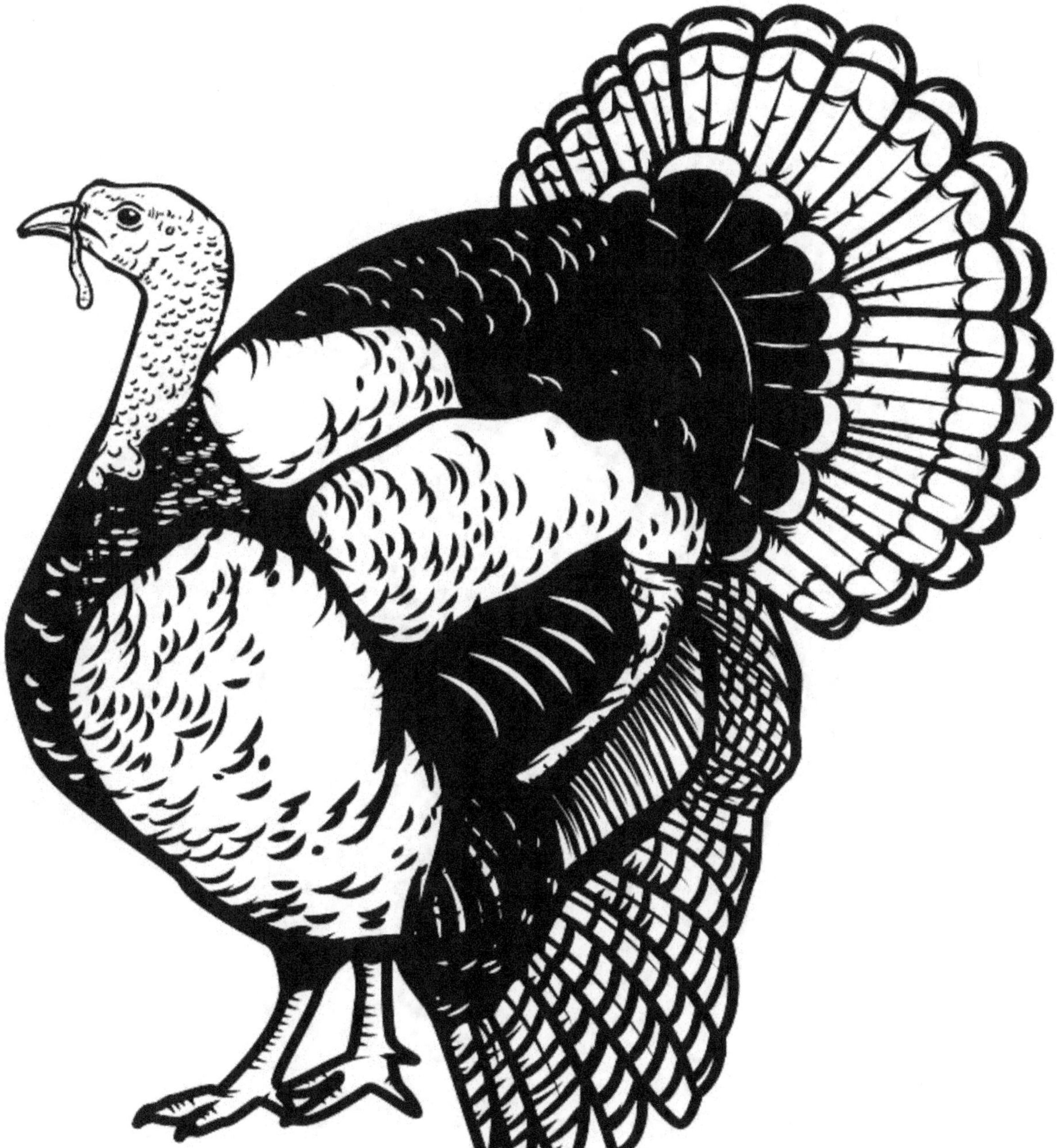

TURKEY COLORING BOOK

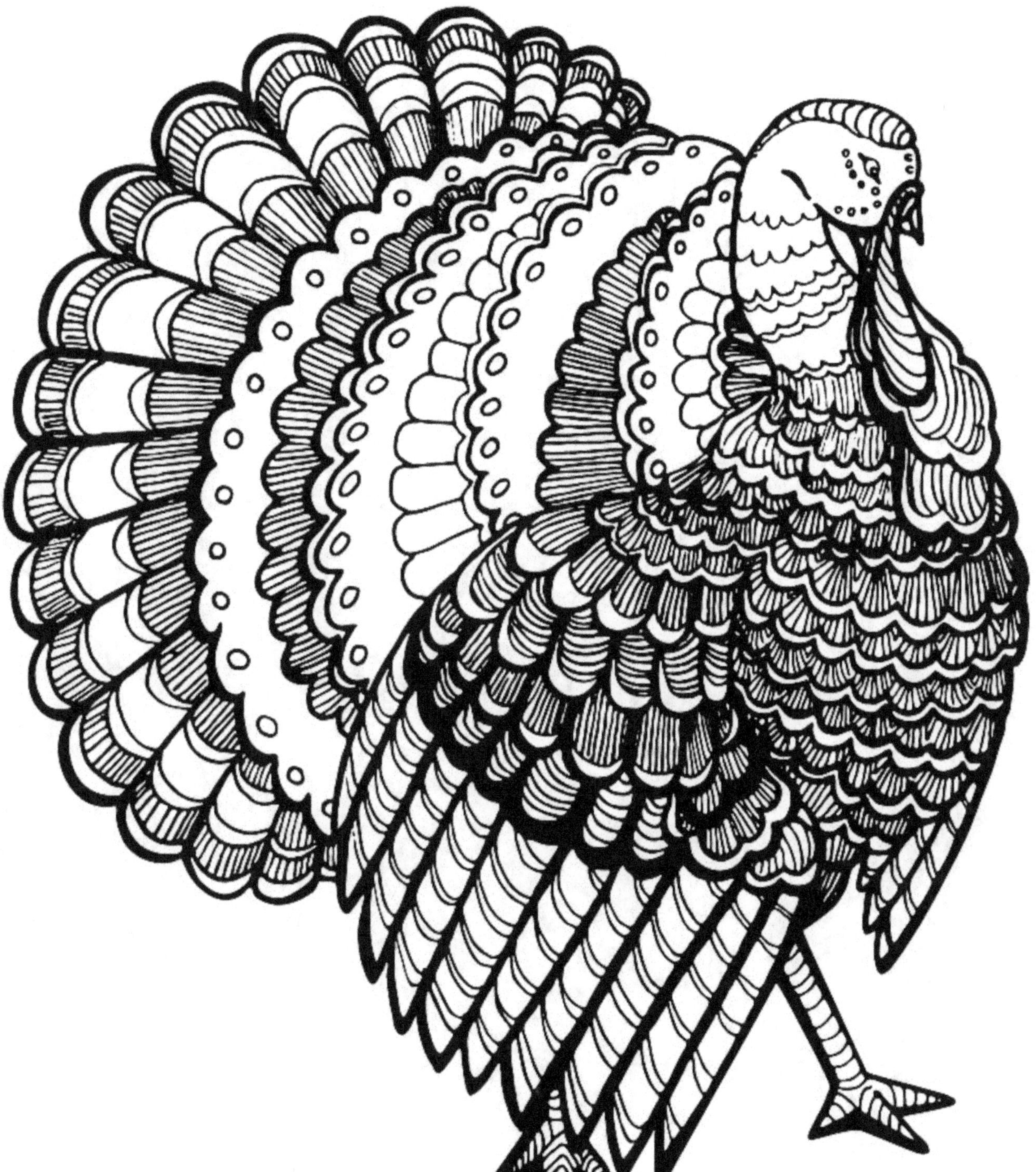

TURKEY COLORING BOOK

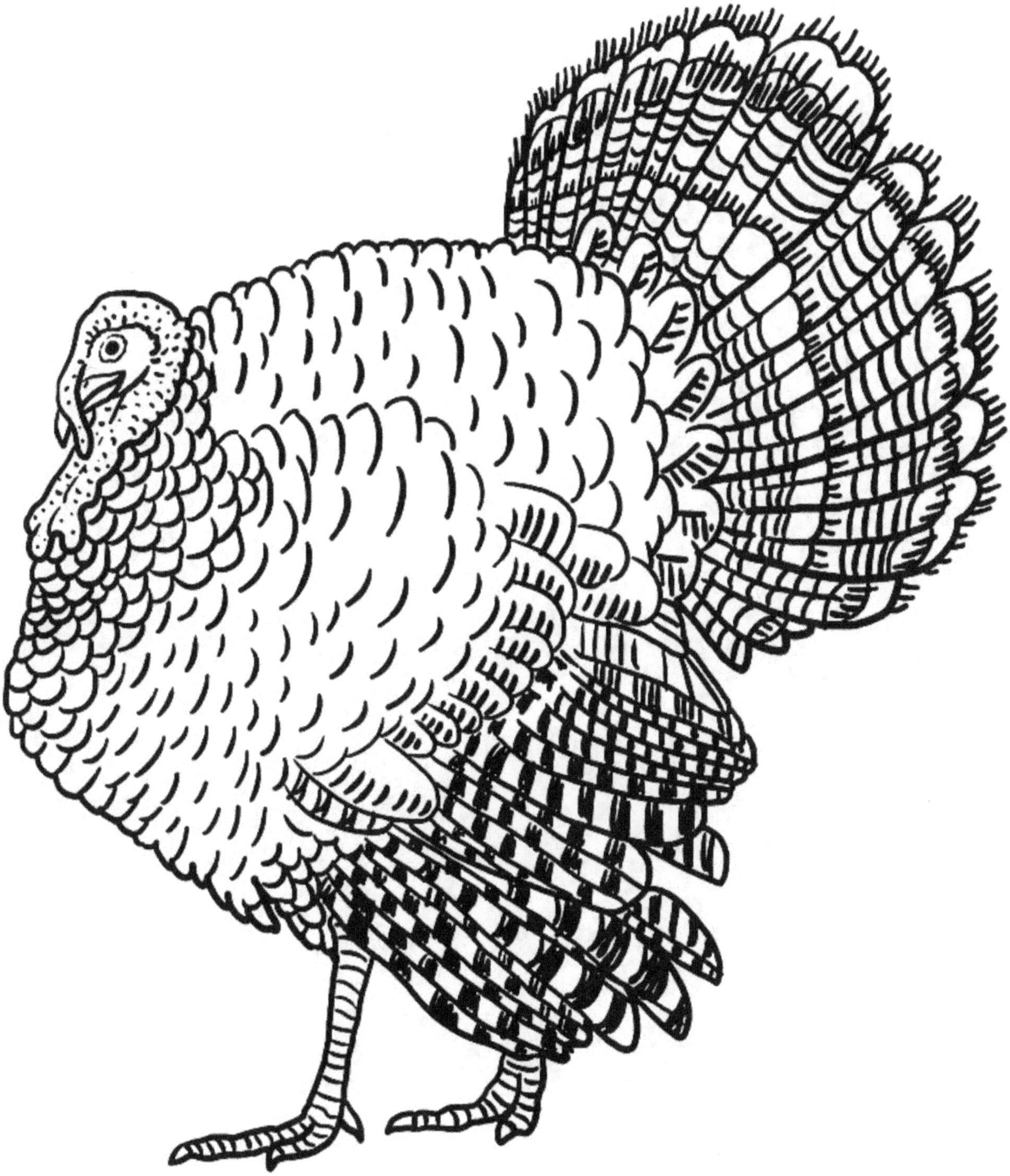

TURKEY COLORING BOOK

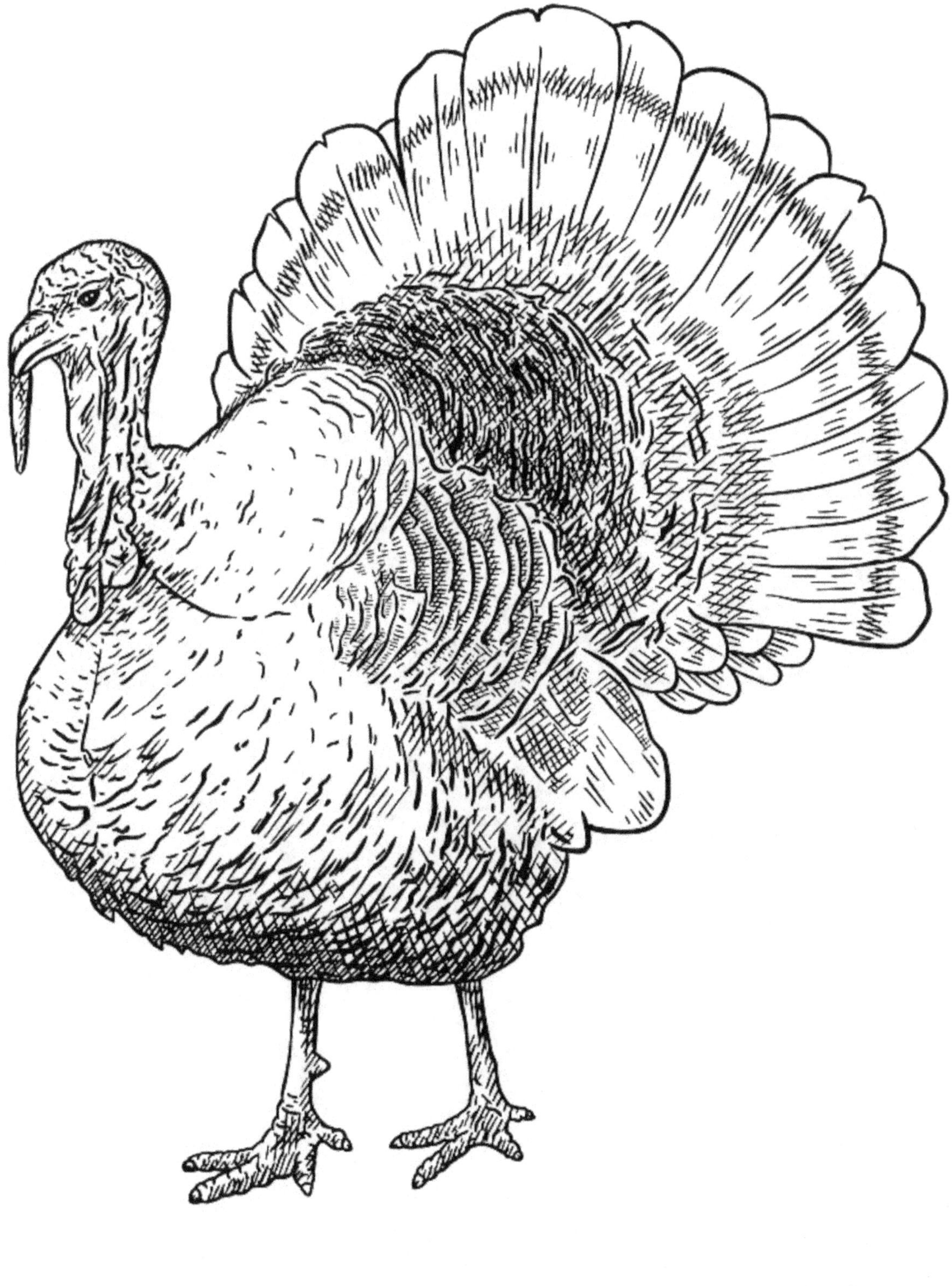

TURKEY COLORING BOOK

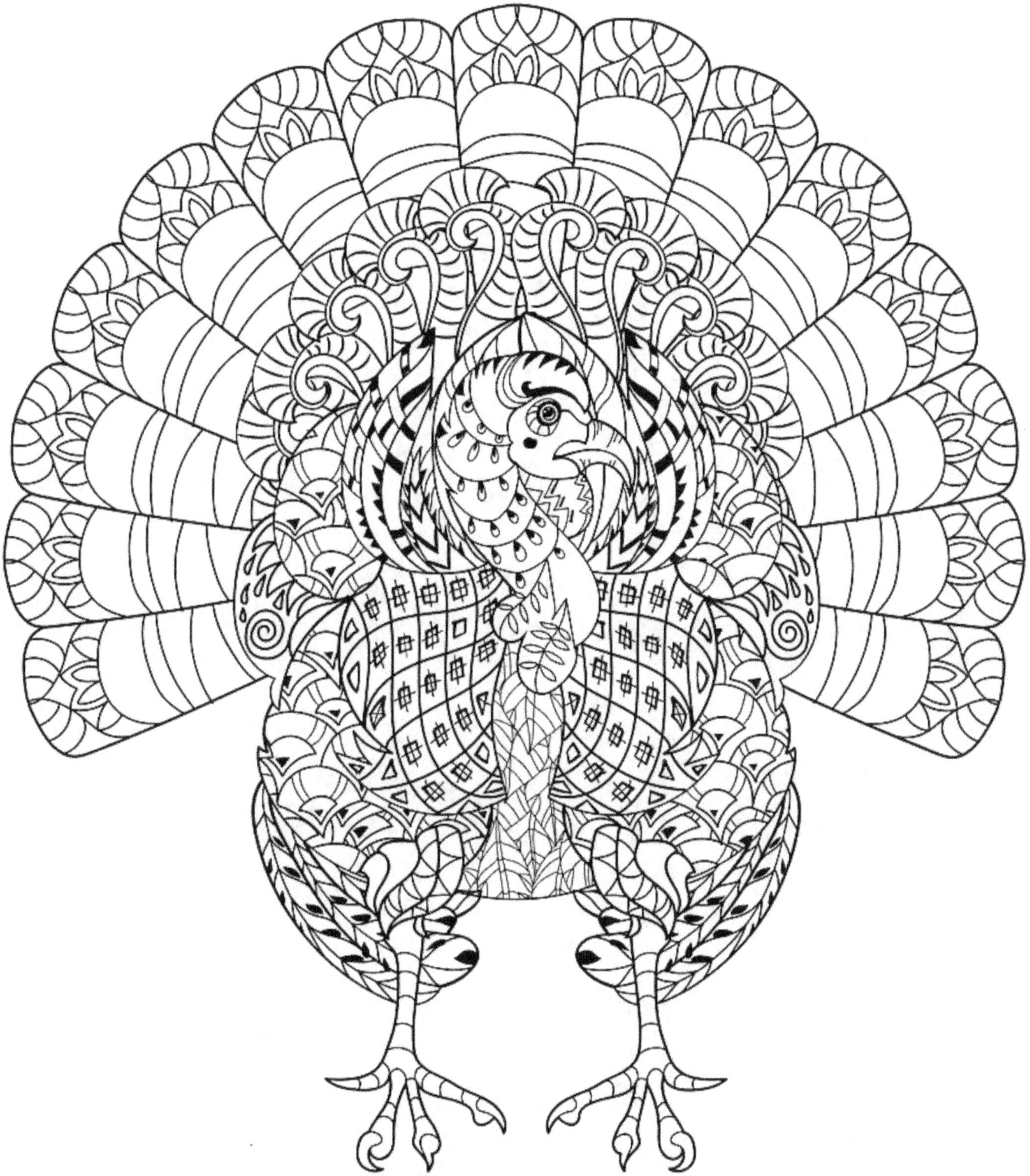

TURKEY COLORING BOOK

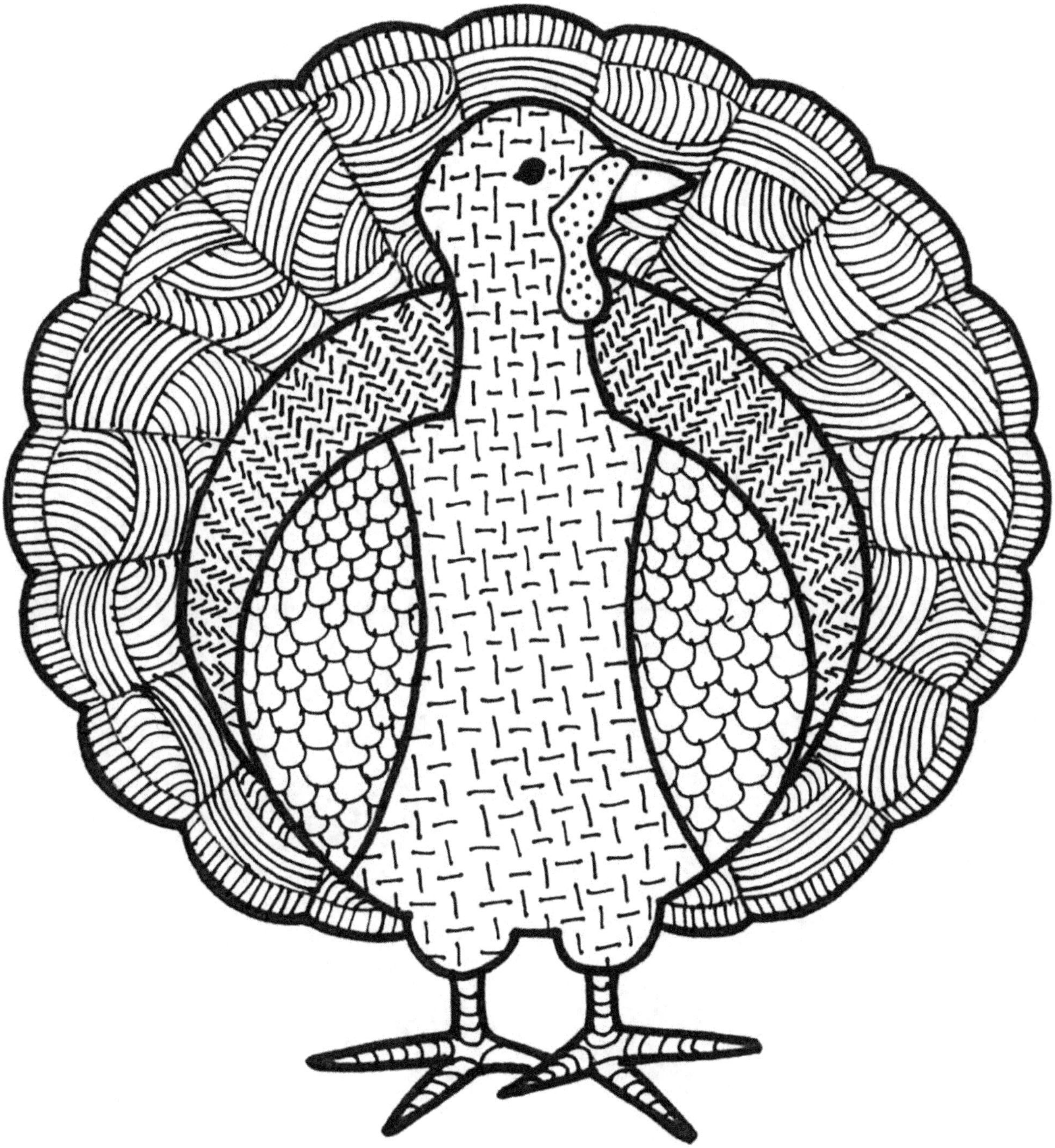

TURKEY COLORING BOOK

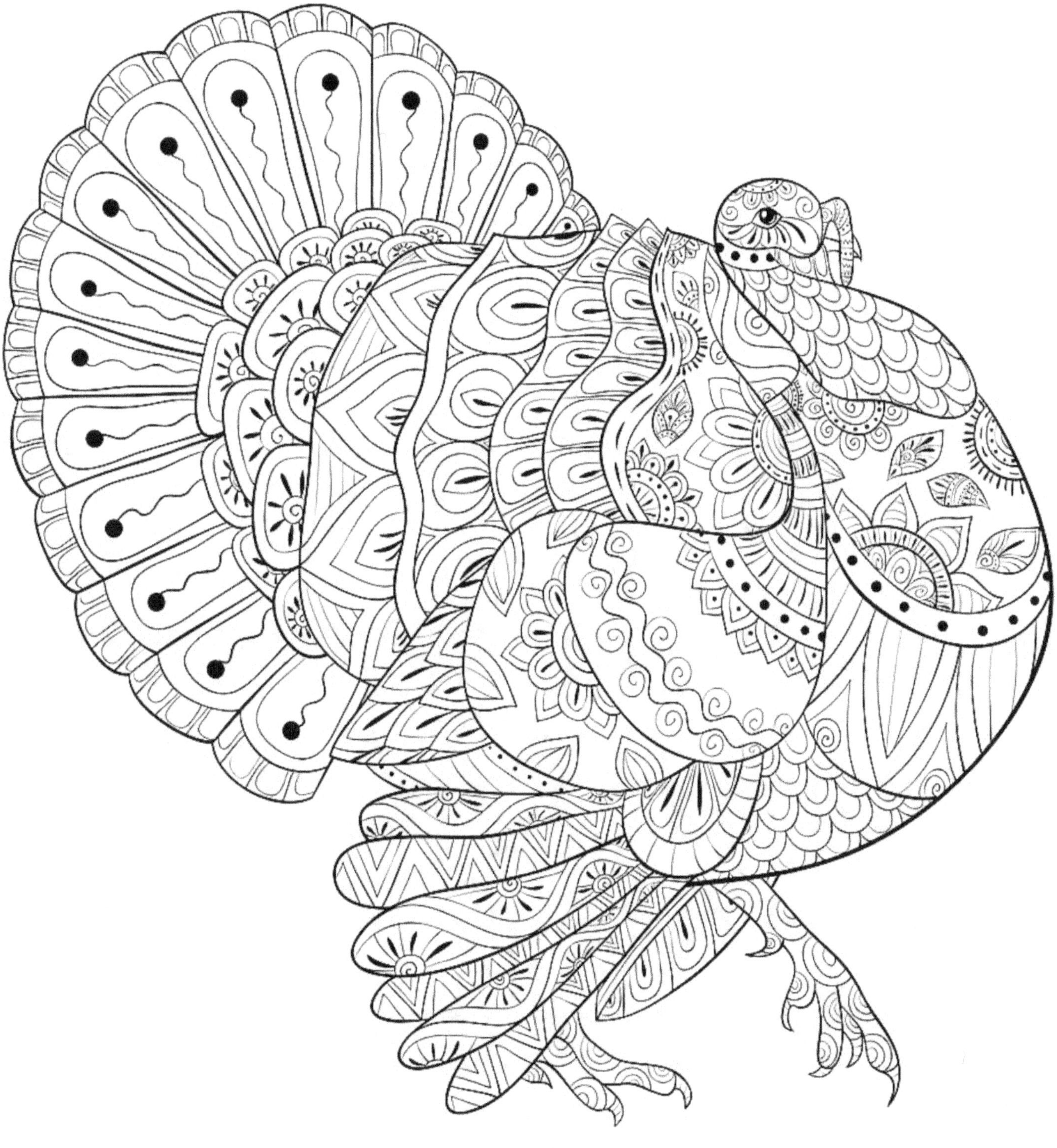

TURKEY COLORING BOOK

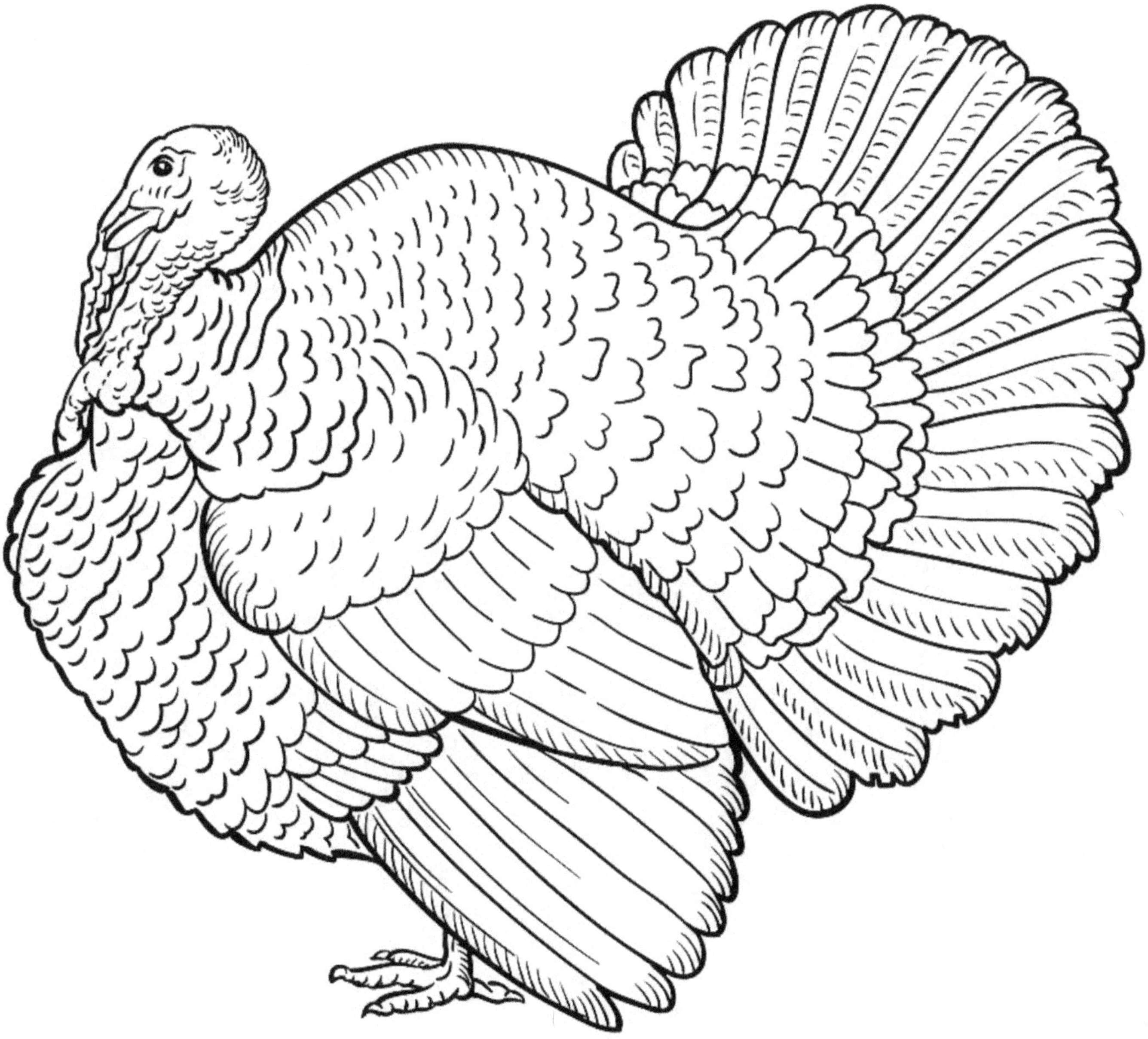

TURKEY COLORING BOOK

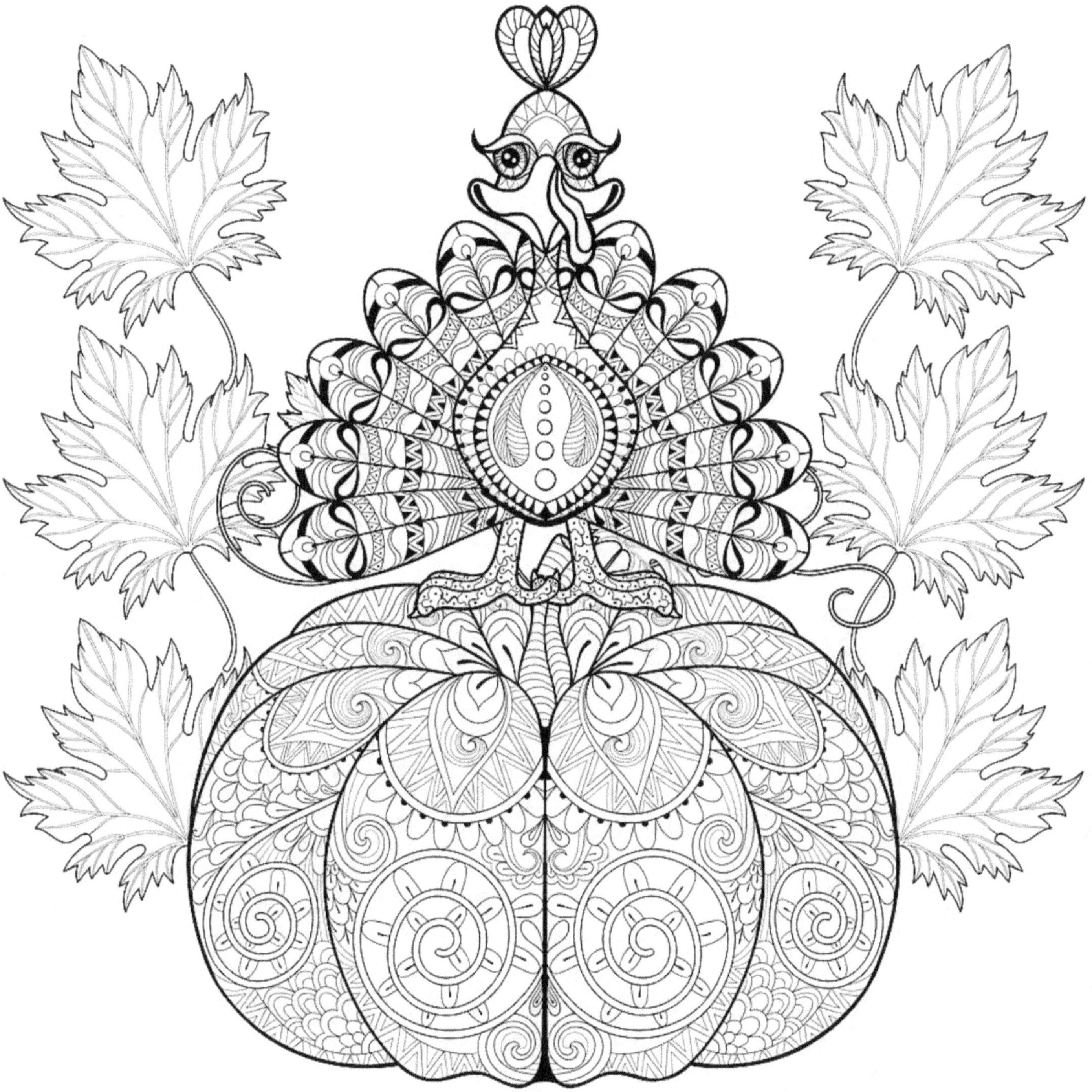

TURKEY COLORING BOOK

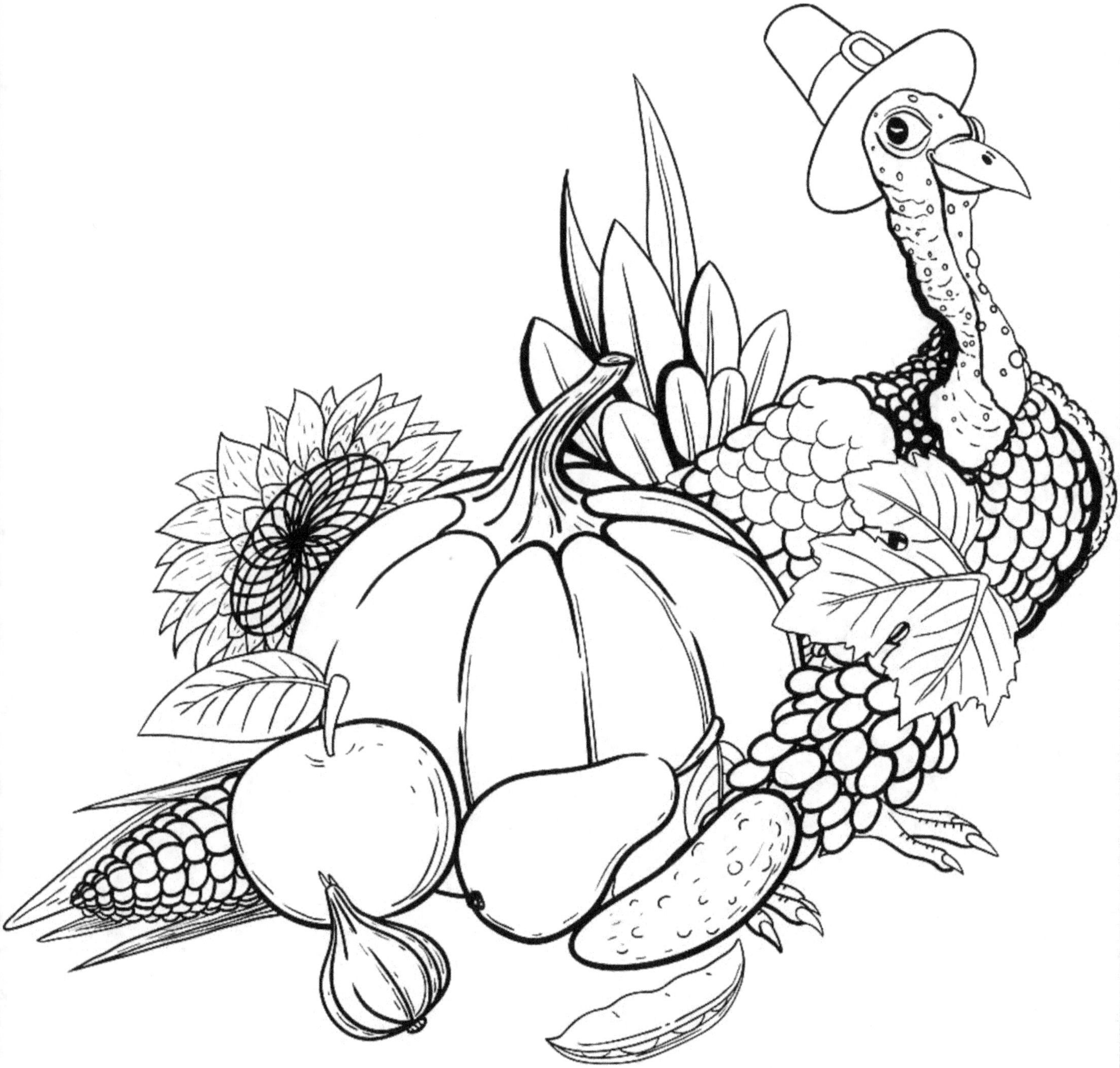

TURKEY COLORING BOOK

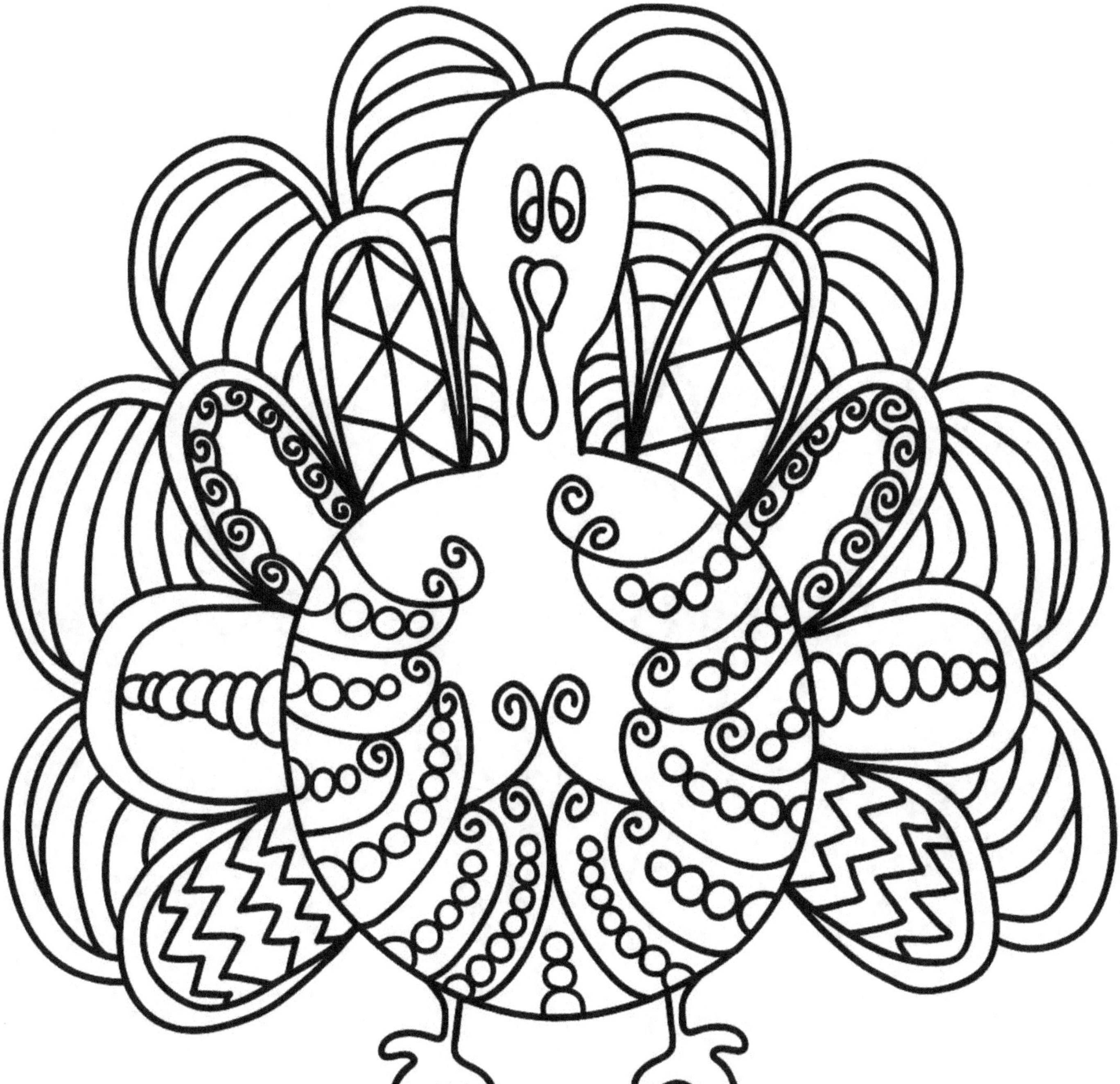

TURKEY COLORING BOOK

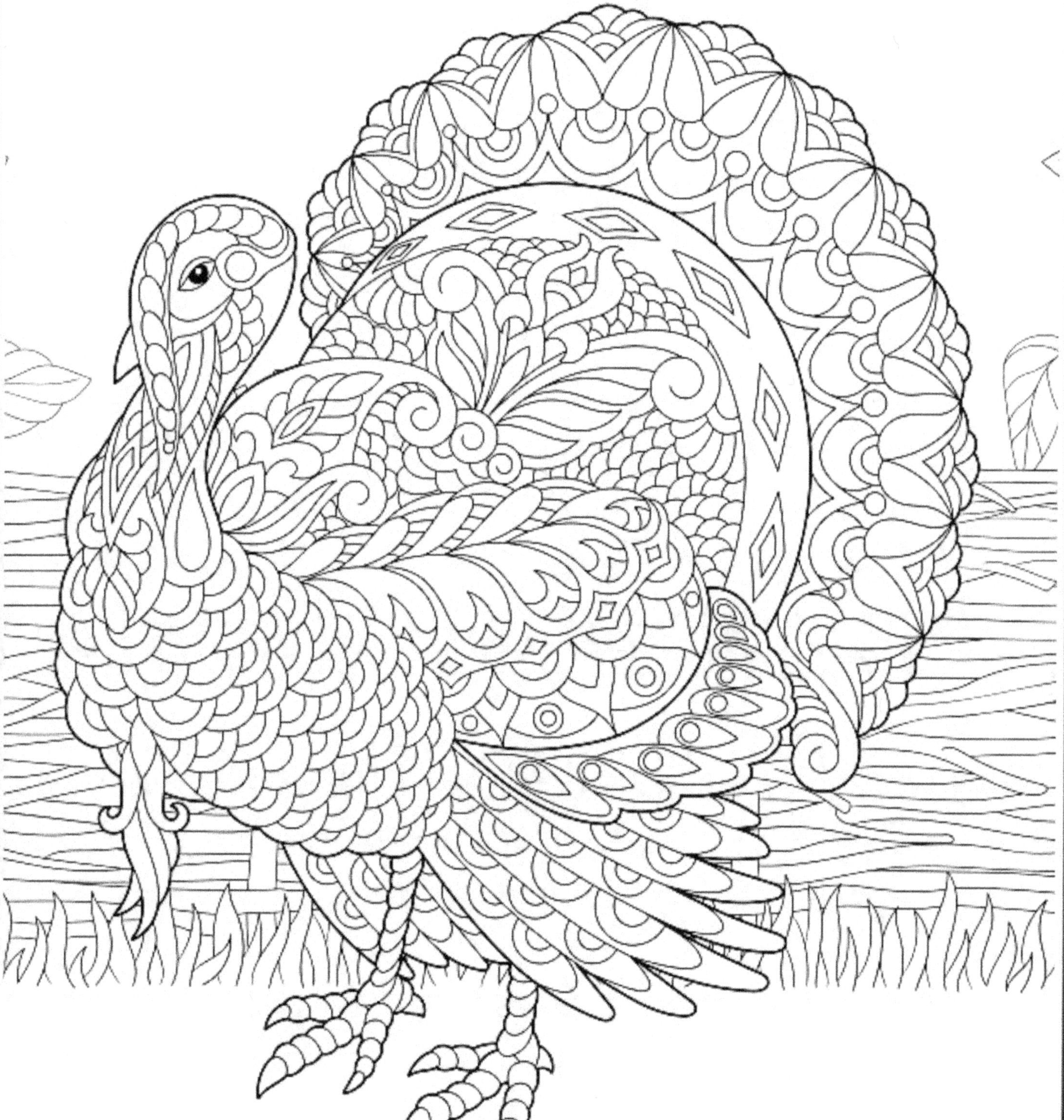

TURKEY COLORING BOOK

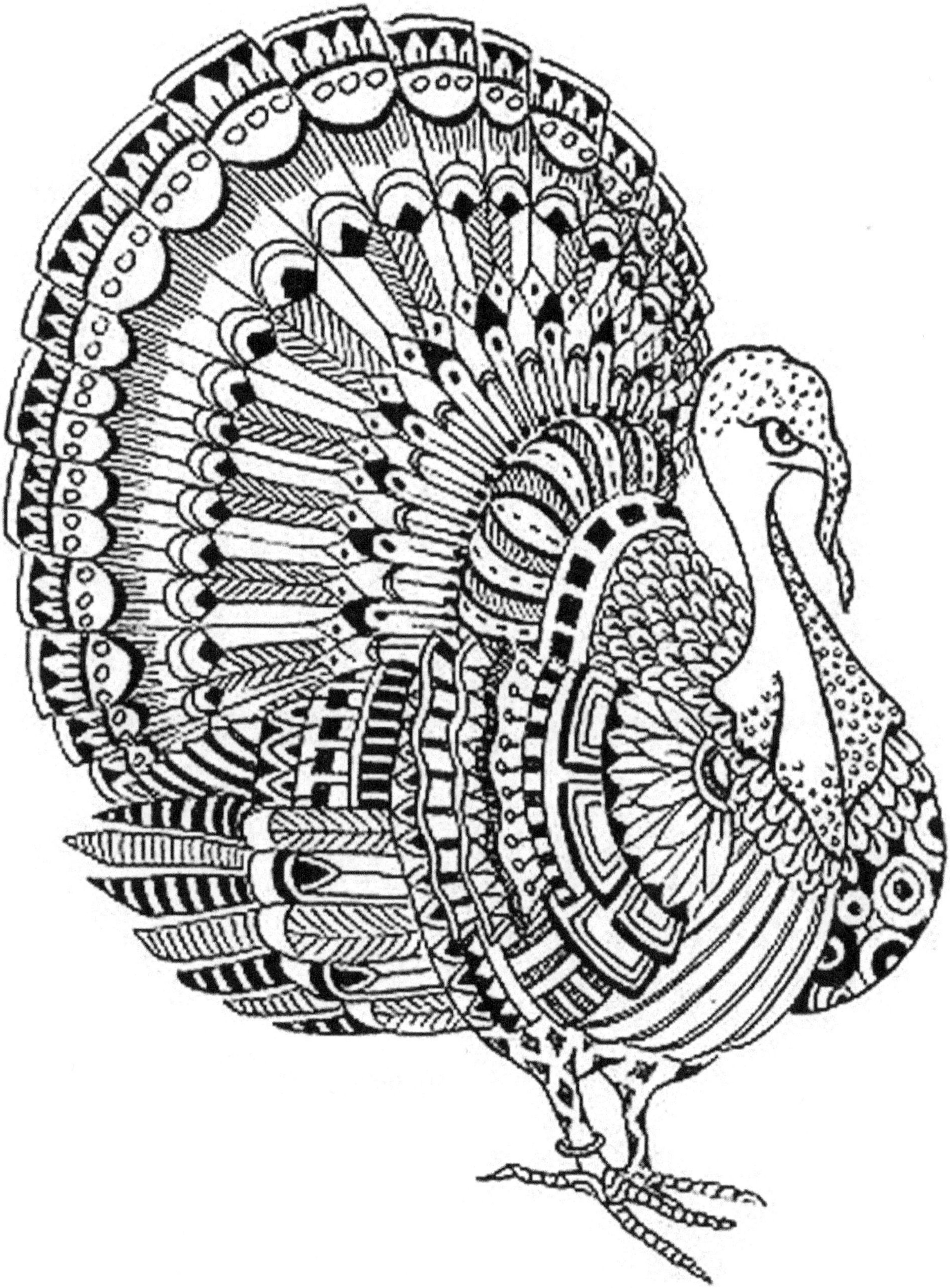

TURKEY COLORING BOOK

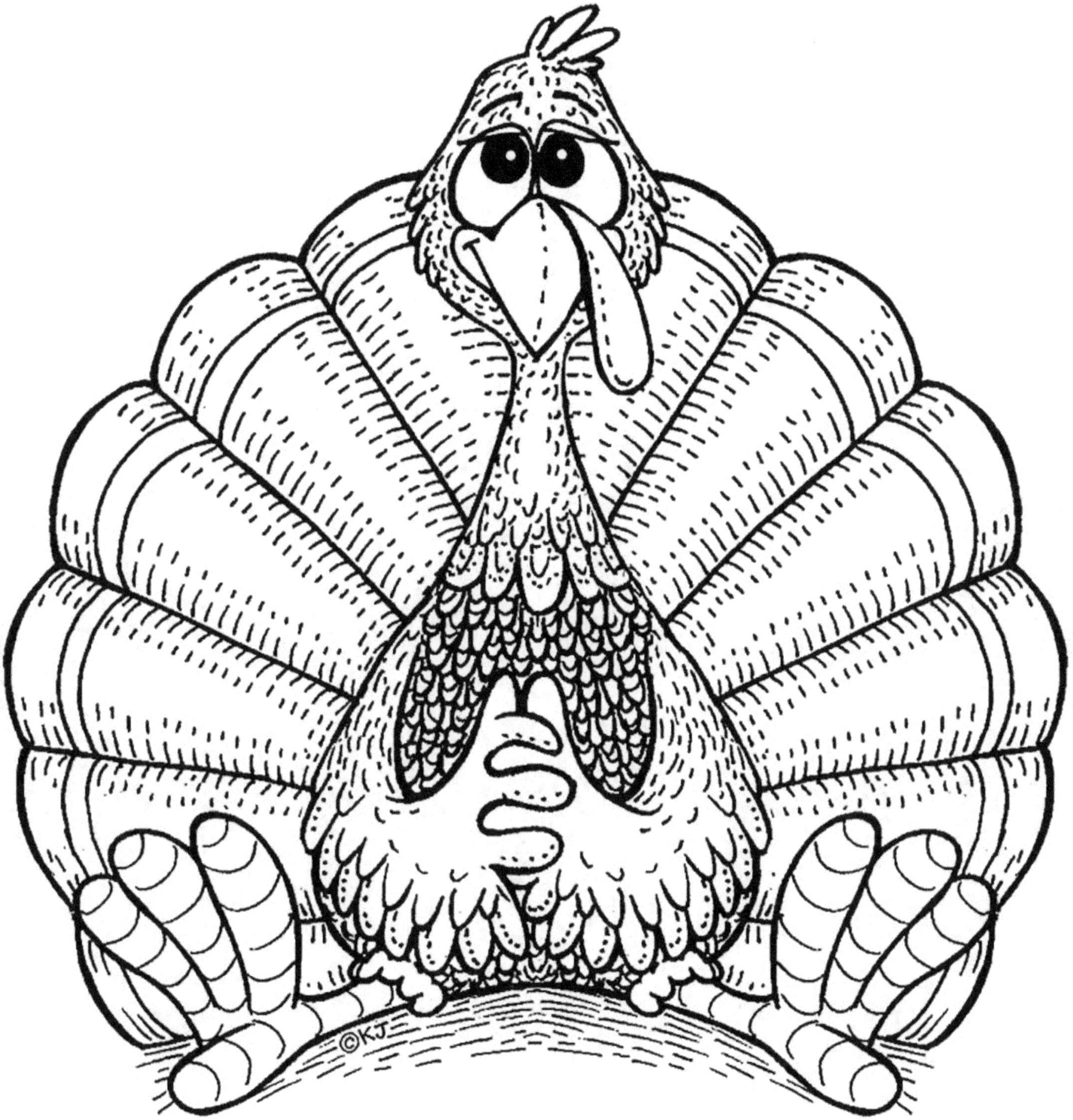

TURKEY COLORING BOOK

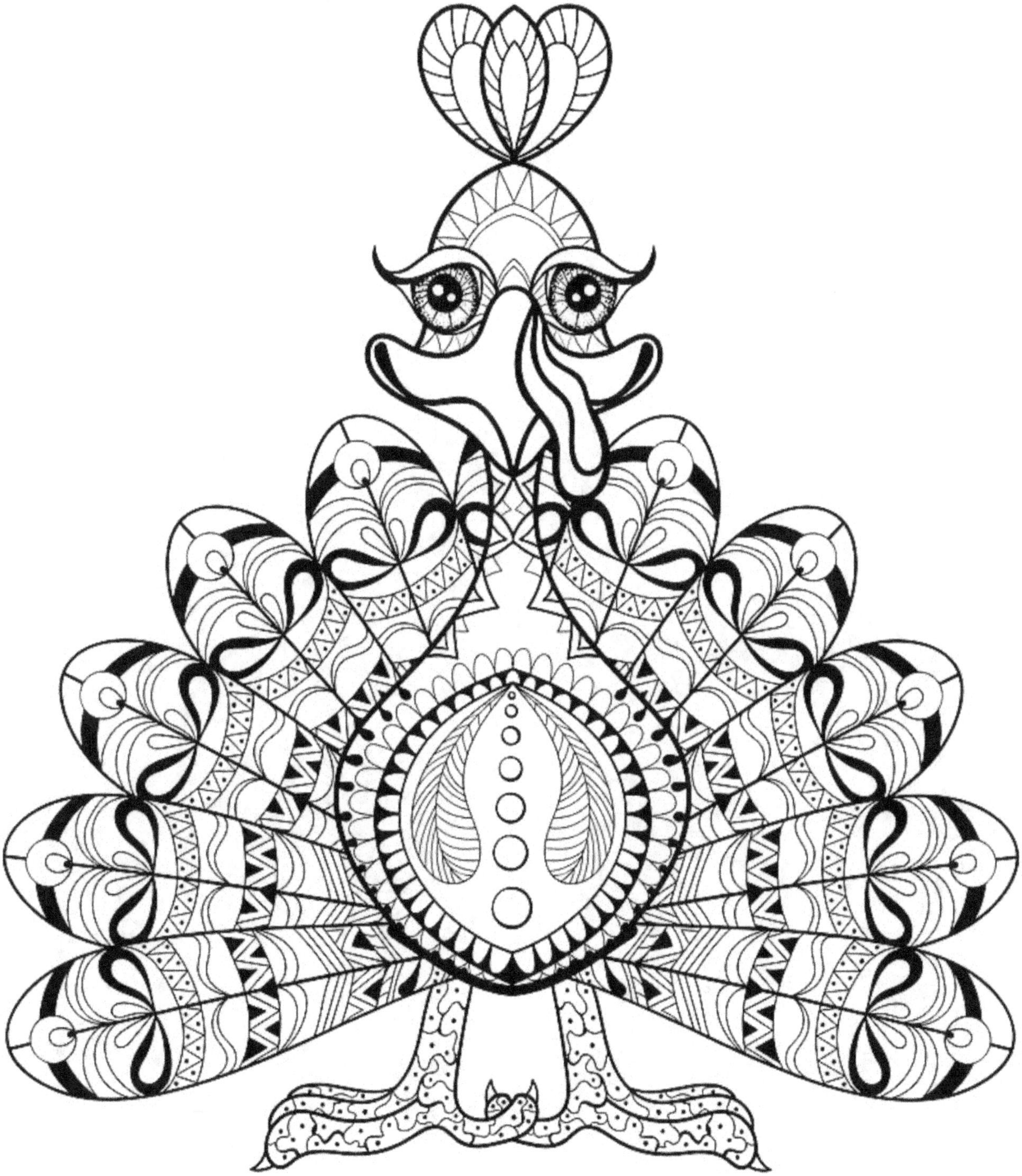

TURKEY COLORING BOOK

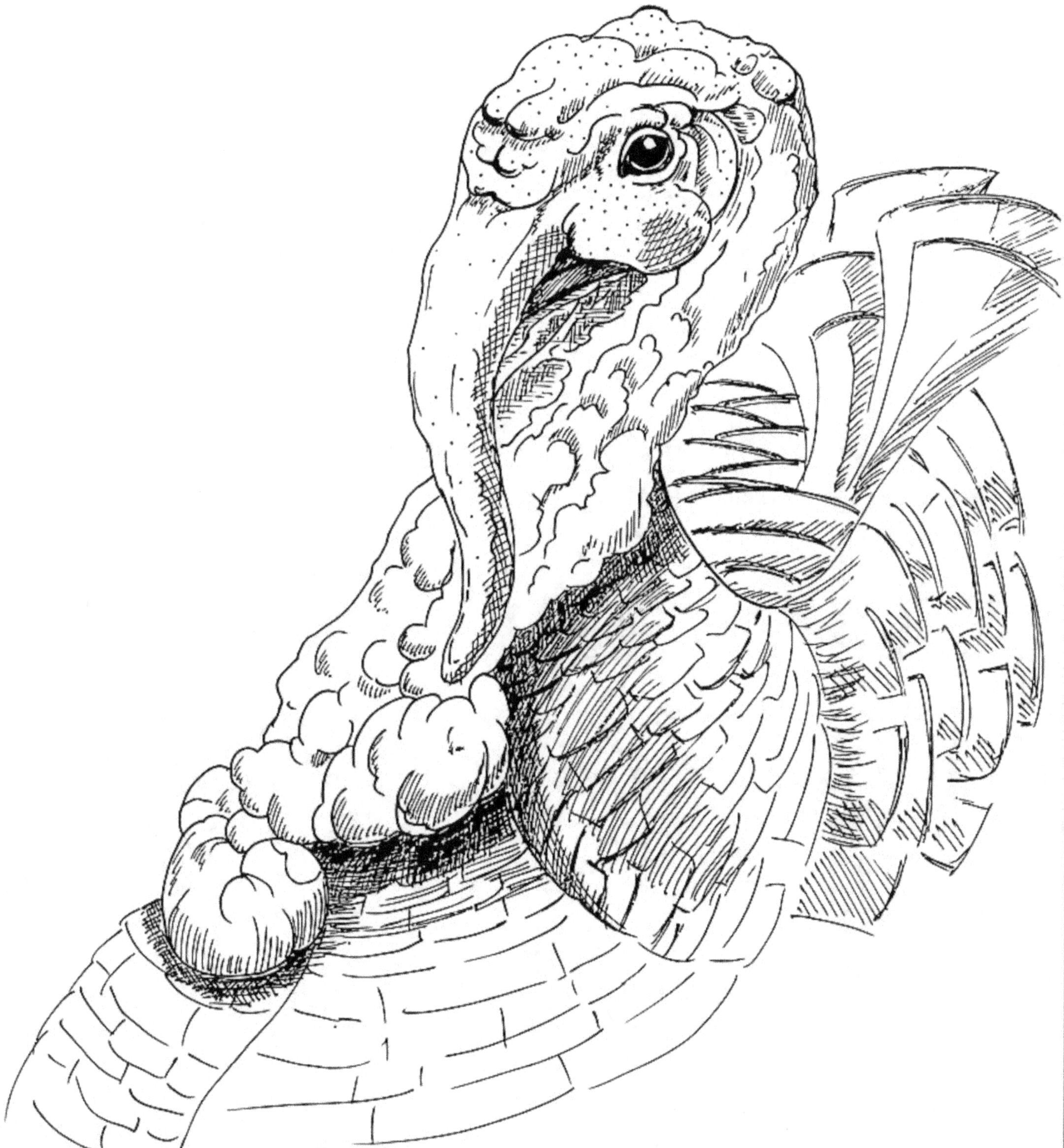

TURKEY COLORING BOOK

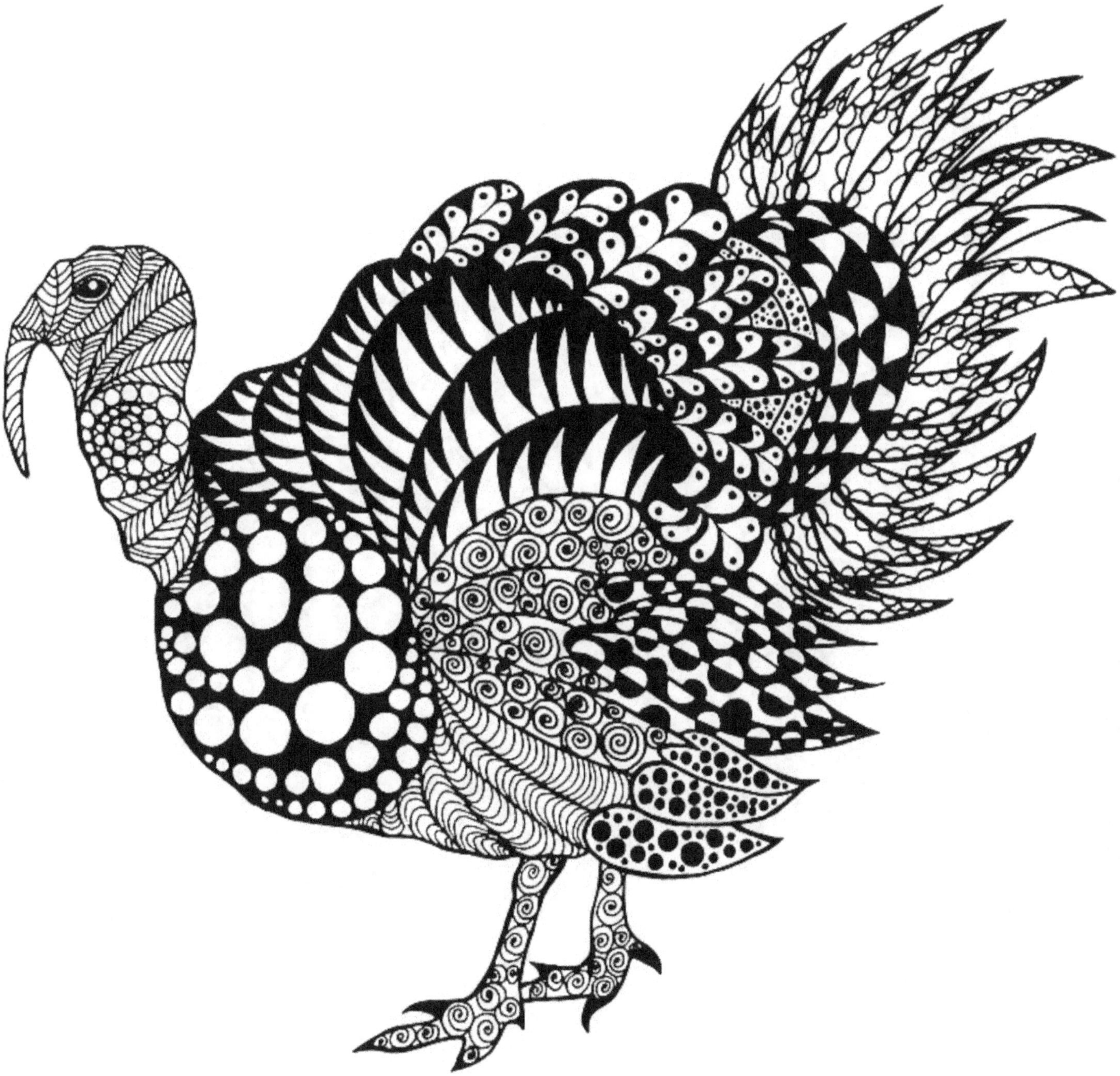

TURKEY COLORING BOOK

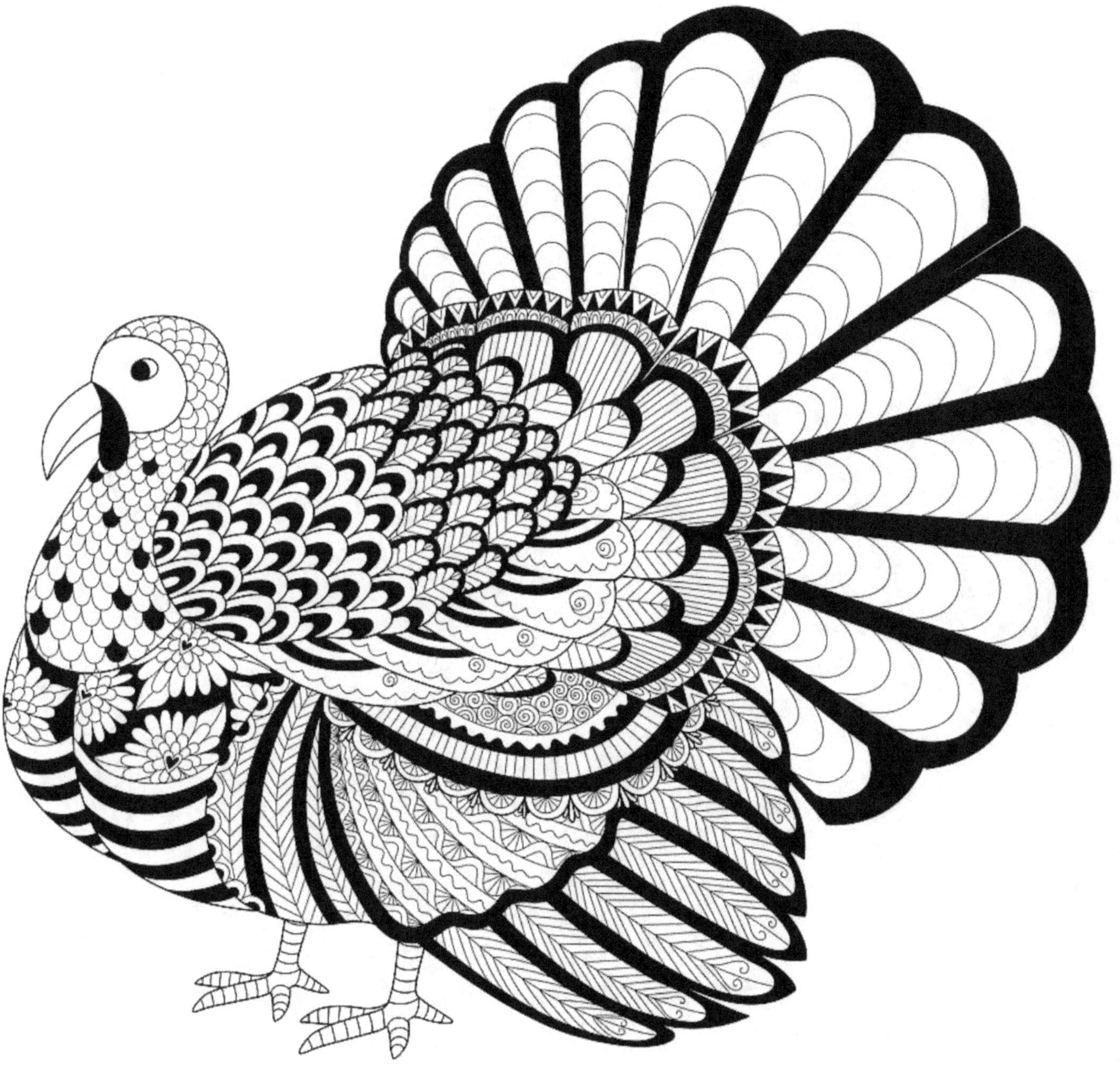

TURKEY COLORING BOOK

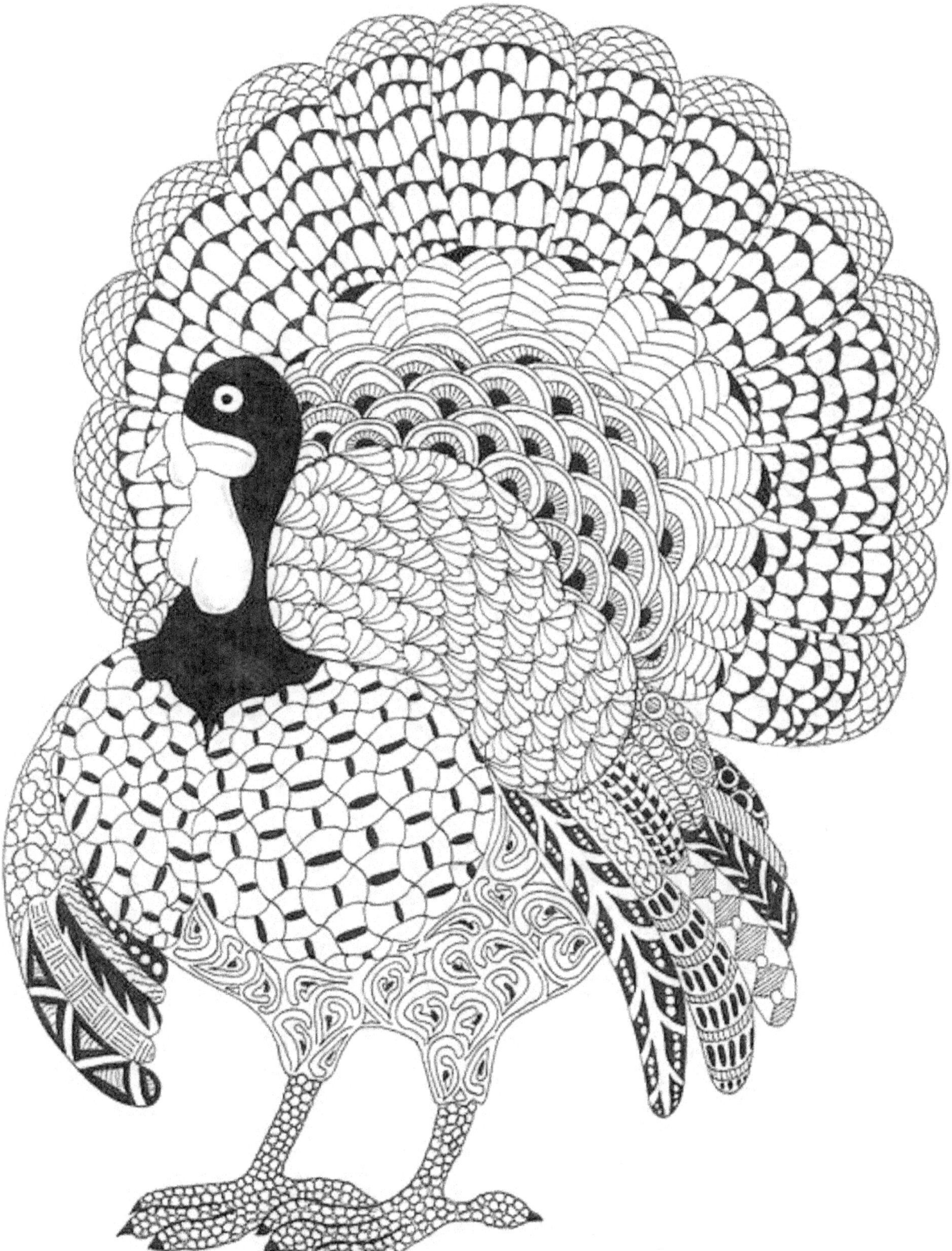

TURKEY COLORING BOOK

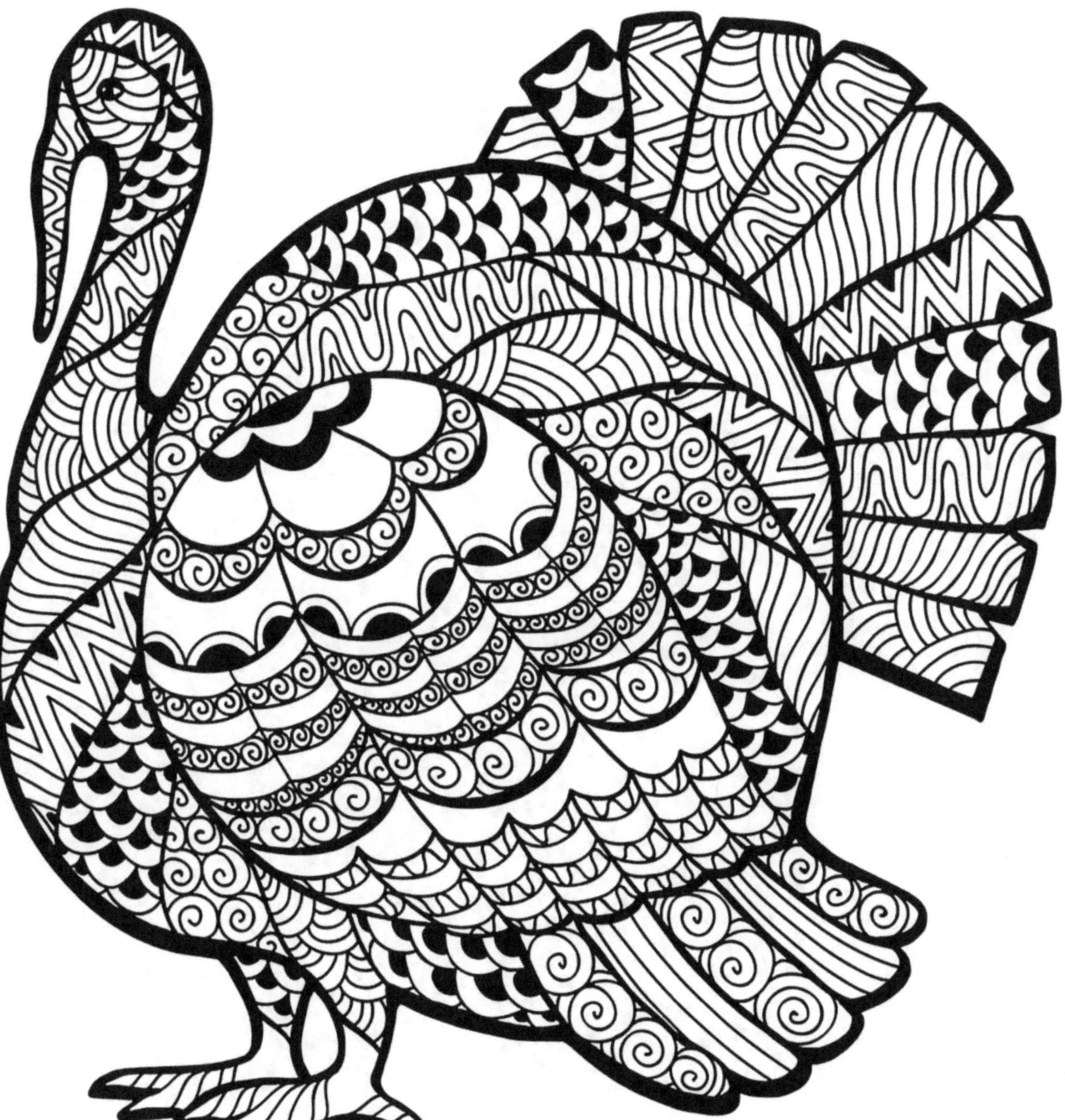

TURKEY COLORING BOOK

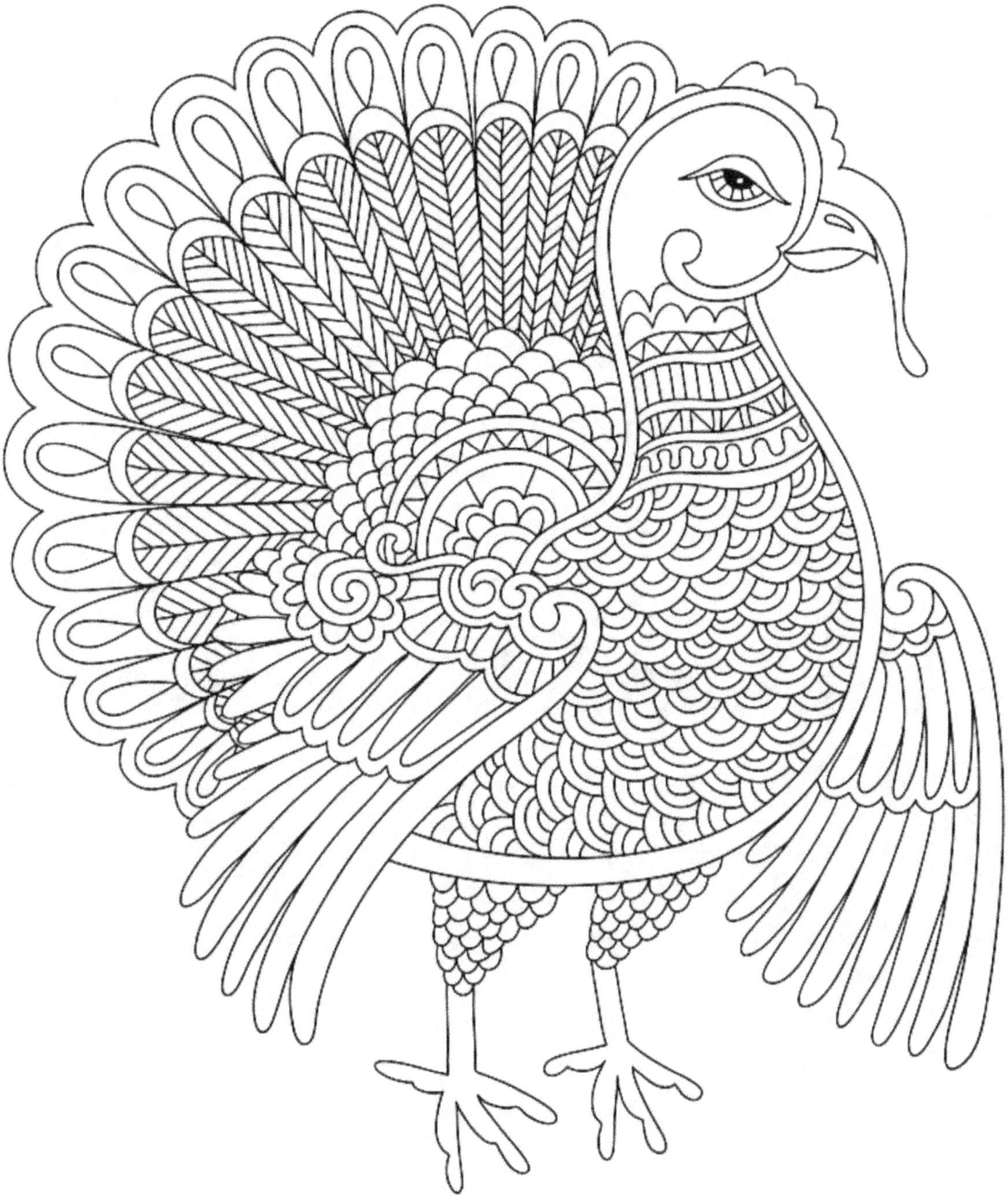

TURKEY COLORING BOOK

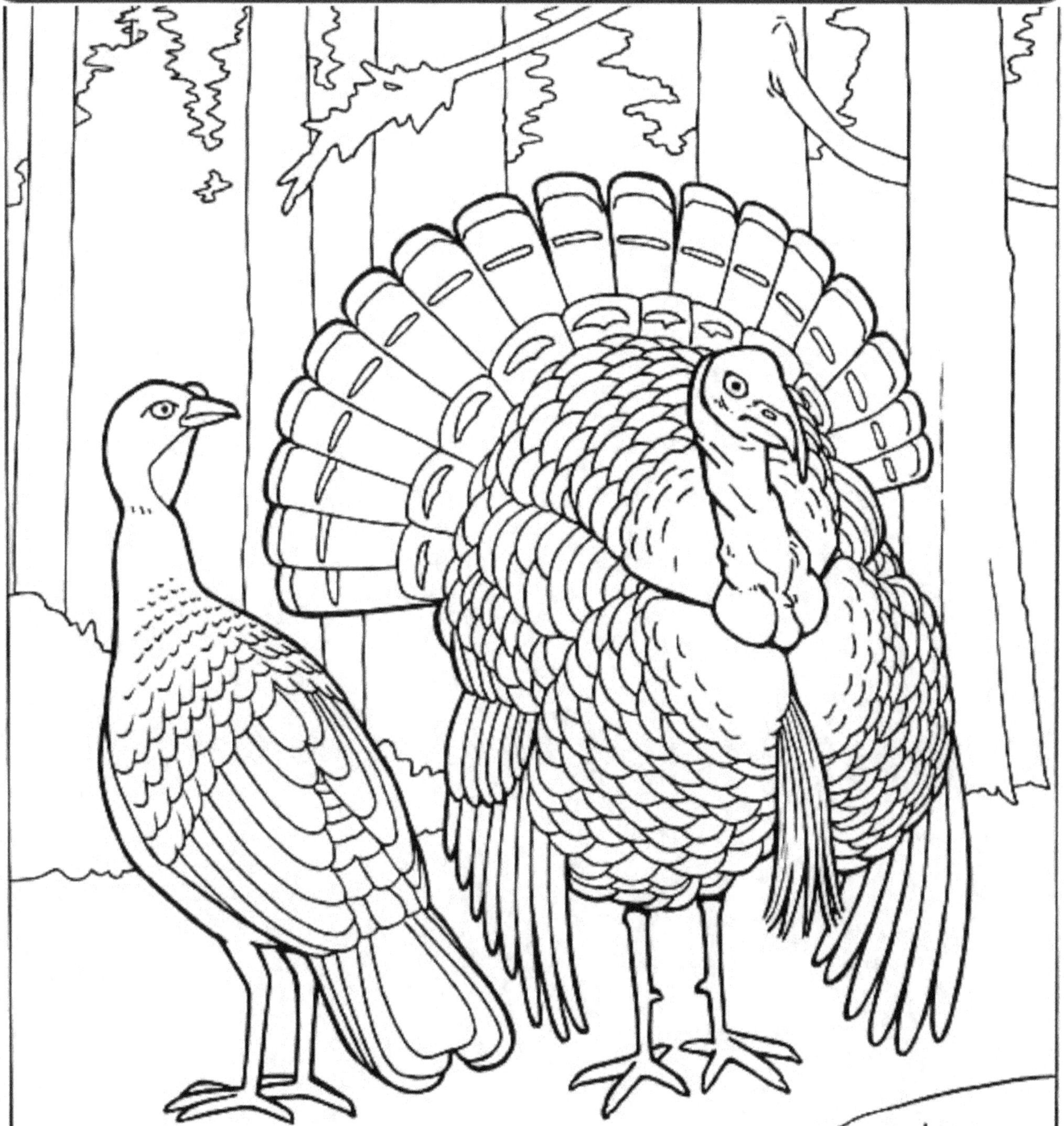

TURKEY COLORING BOOK

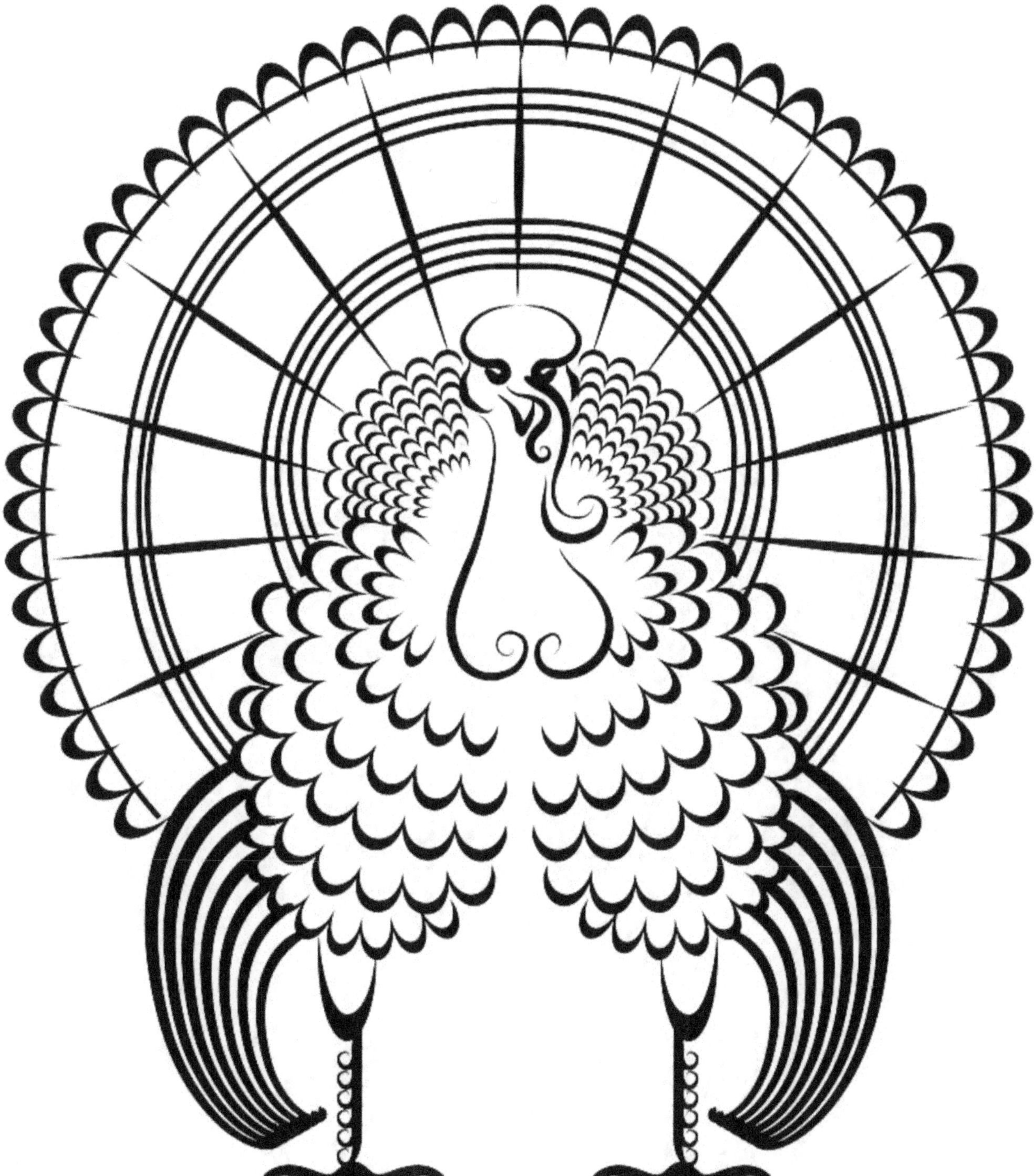

TURKEY COLORING BOOK

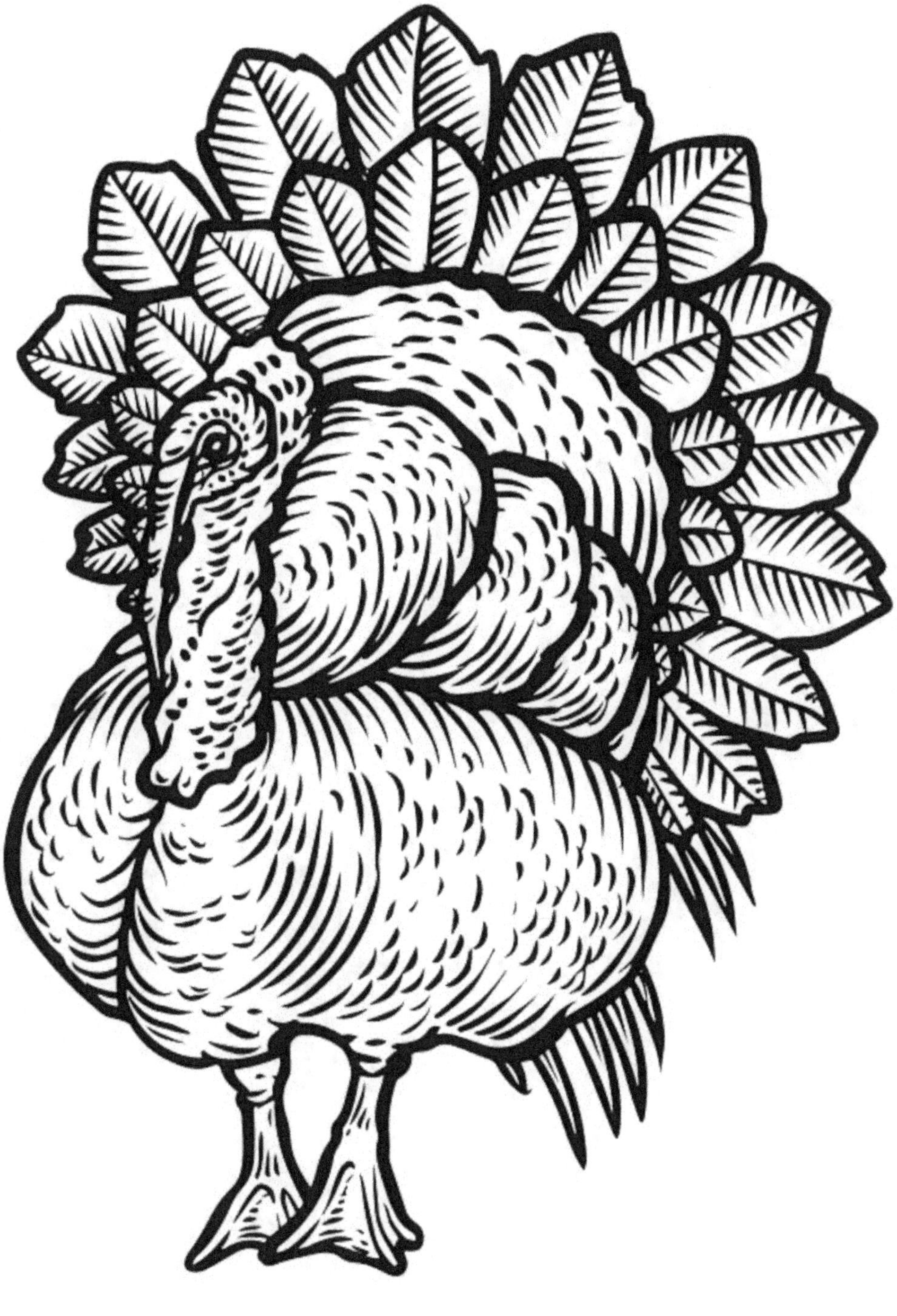

TURKEY COLORING BOOK

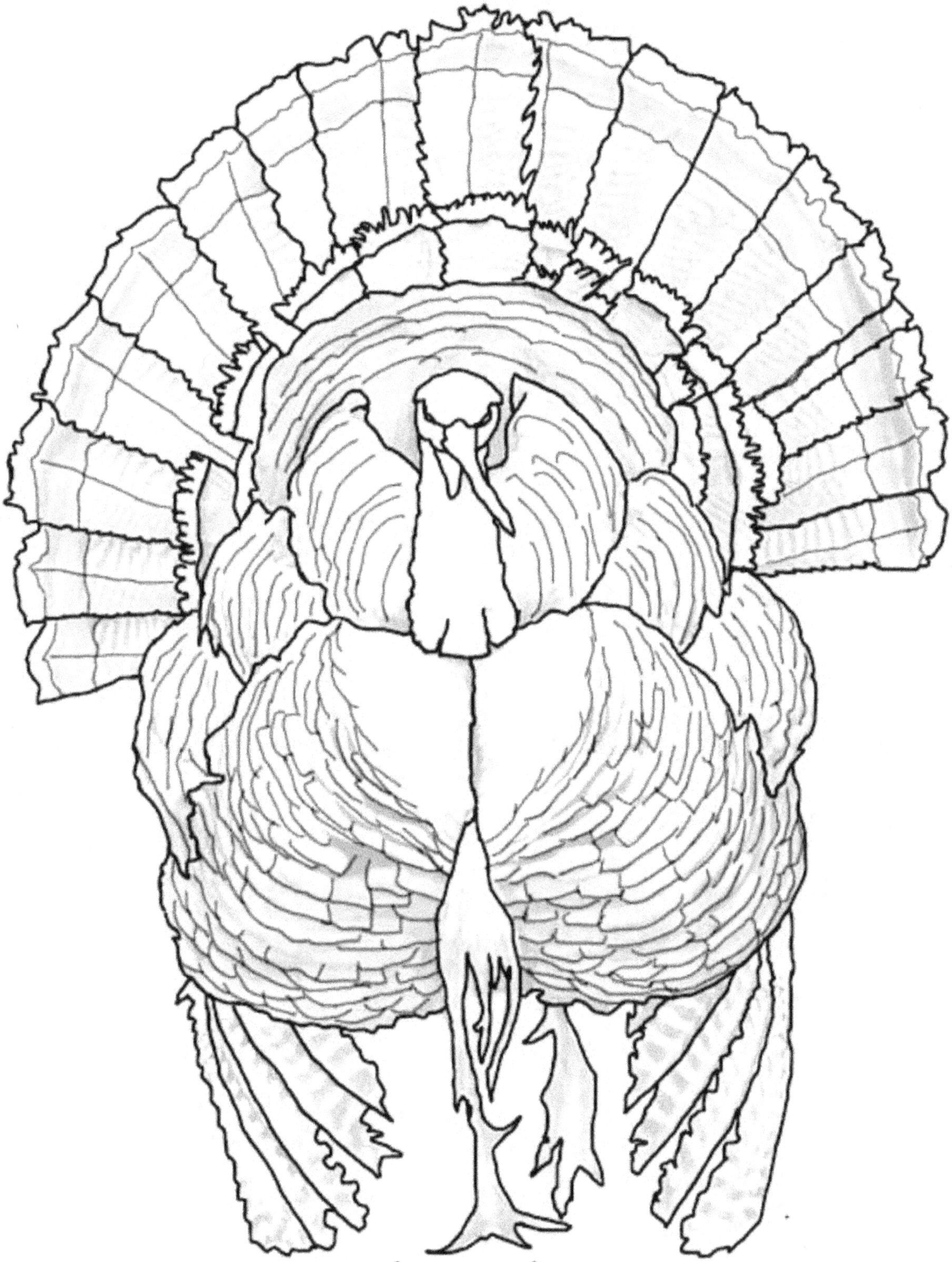

TURKEY COLORING BOOK

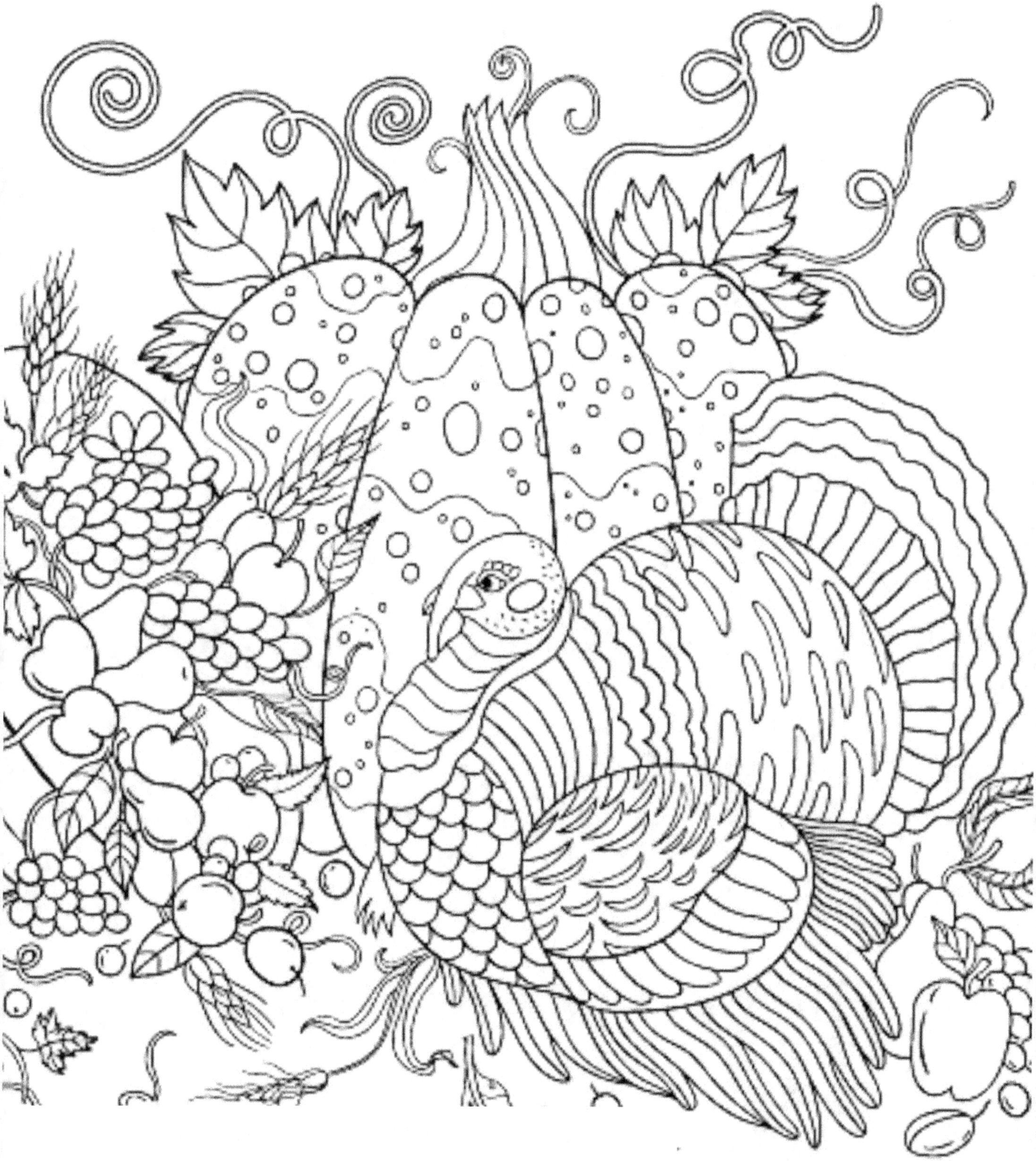

TURKEY COLORING BOOK

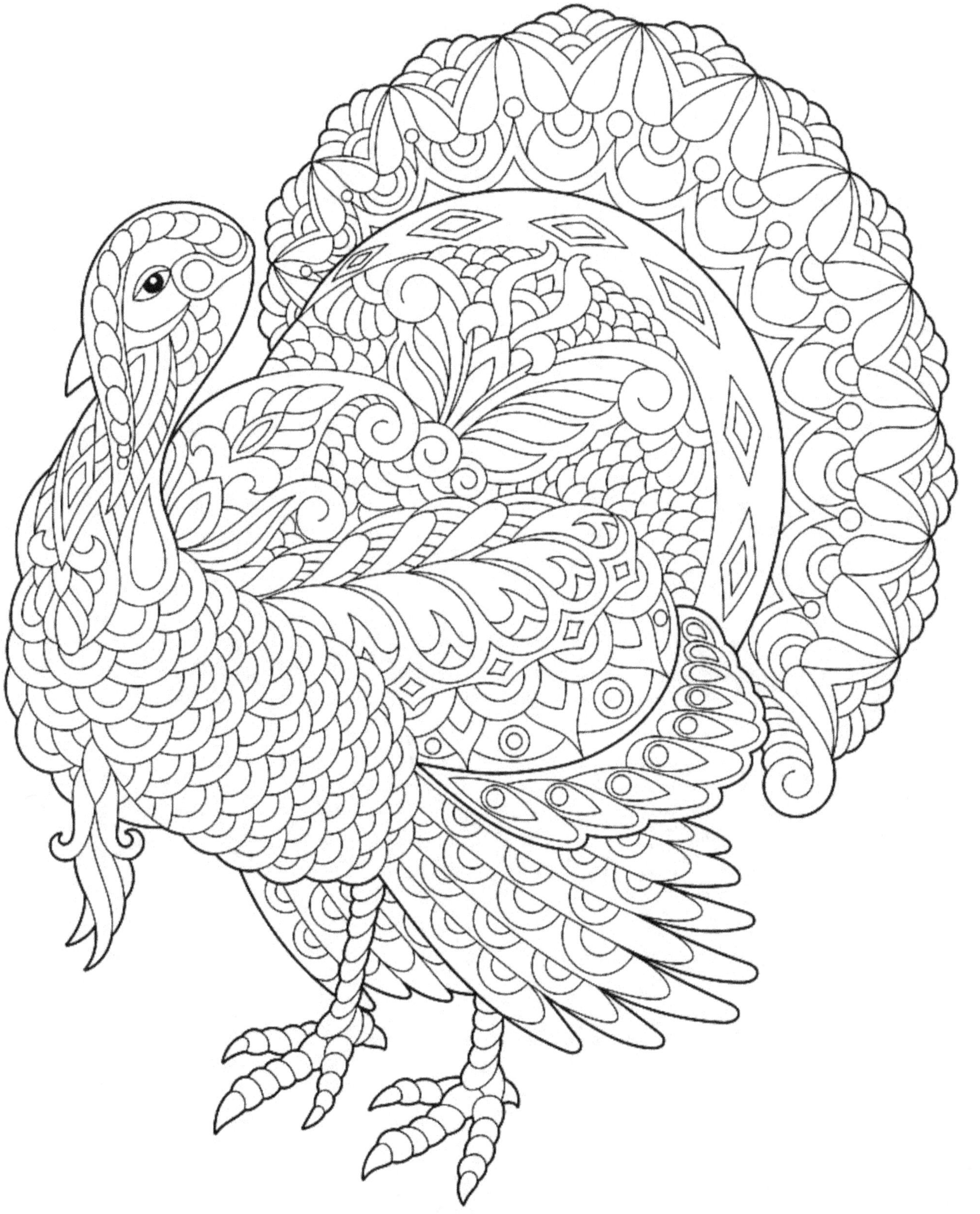

TURKEY COLORING BOOK

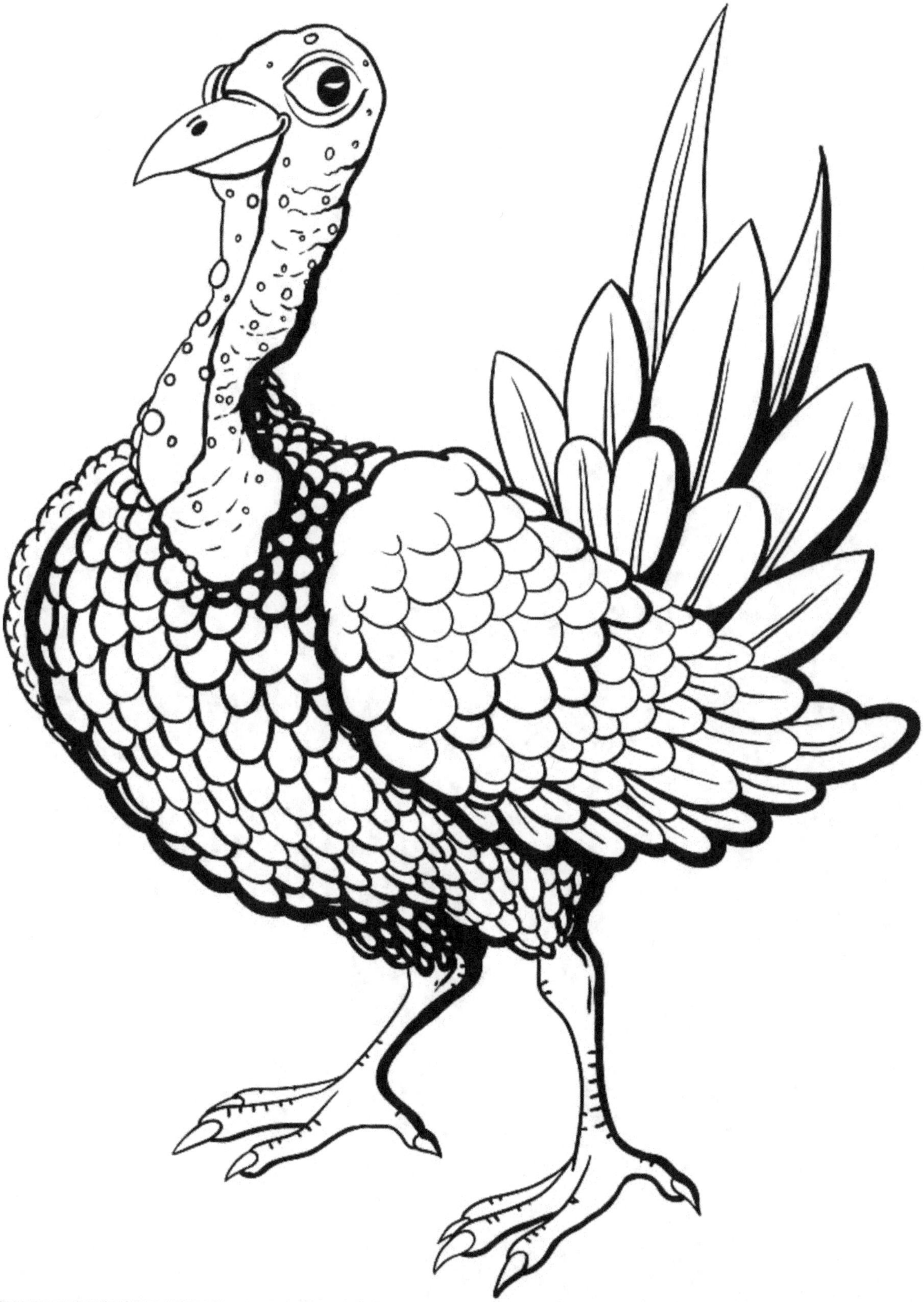

TURKEY COLORING BOOK

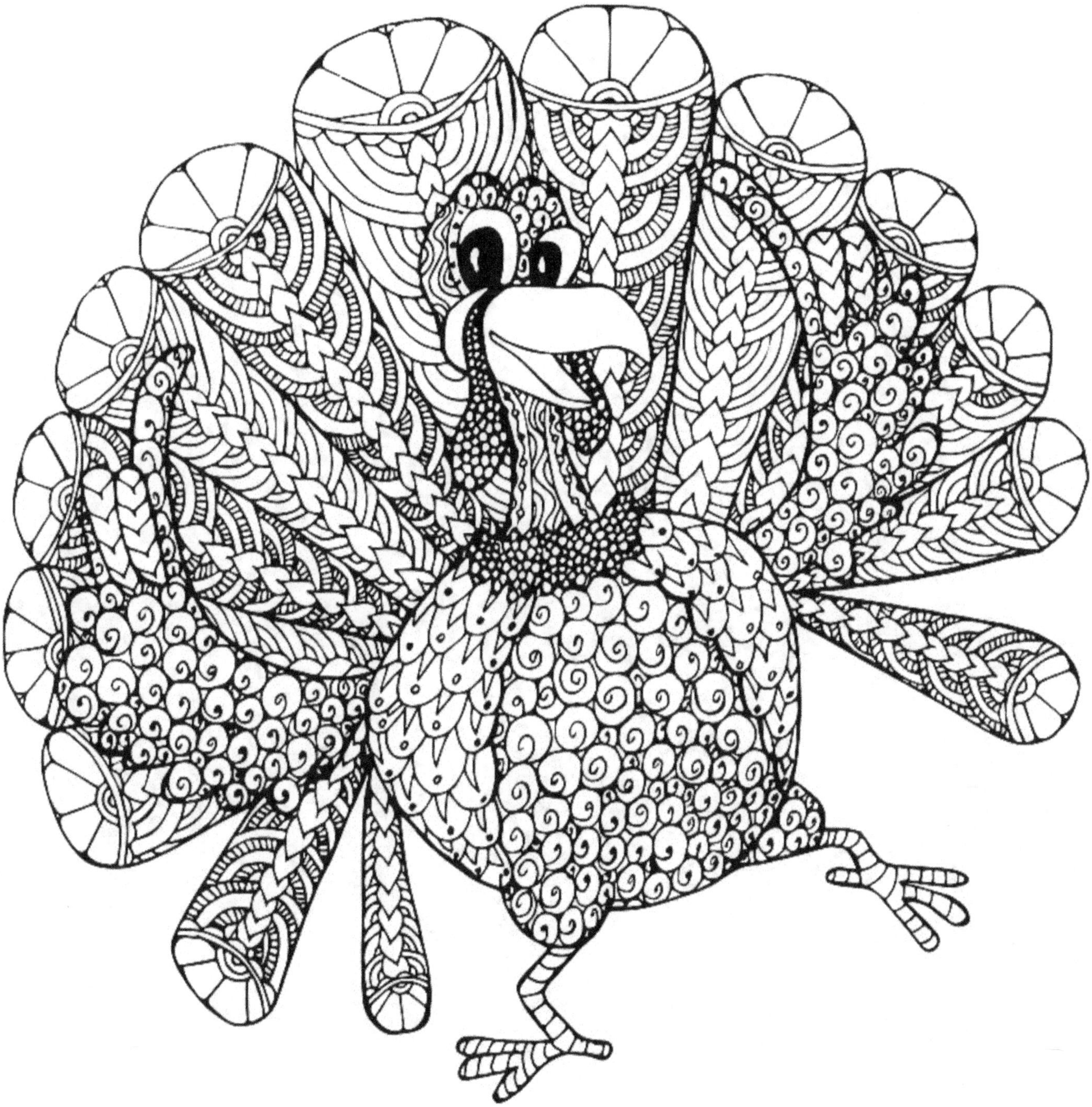

TURKEY COLORING BOOK

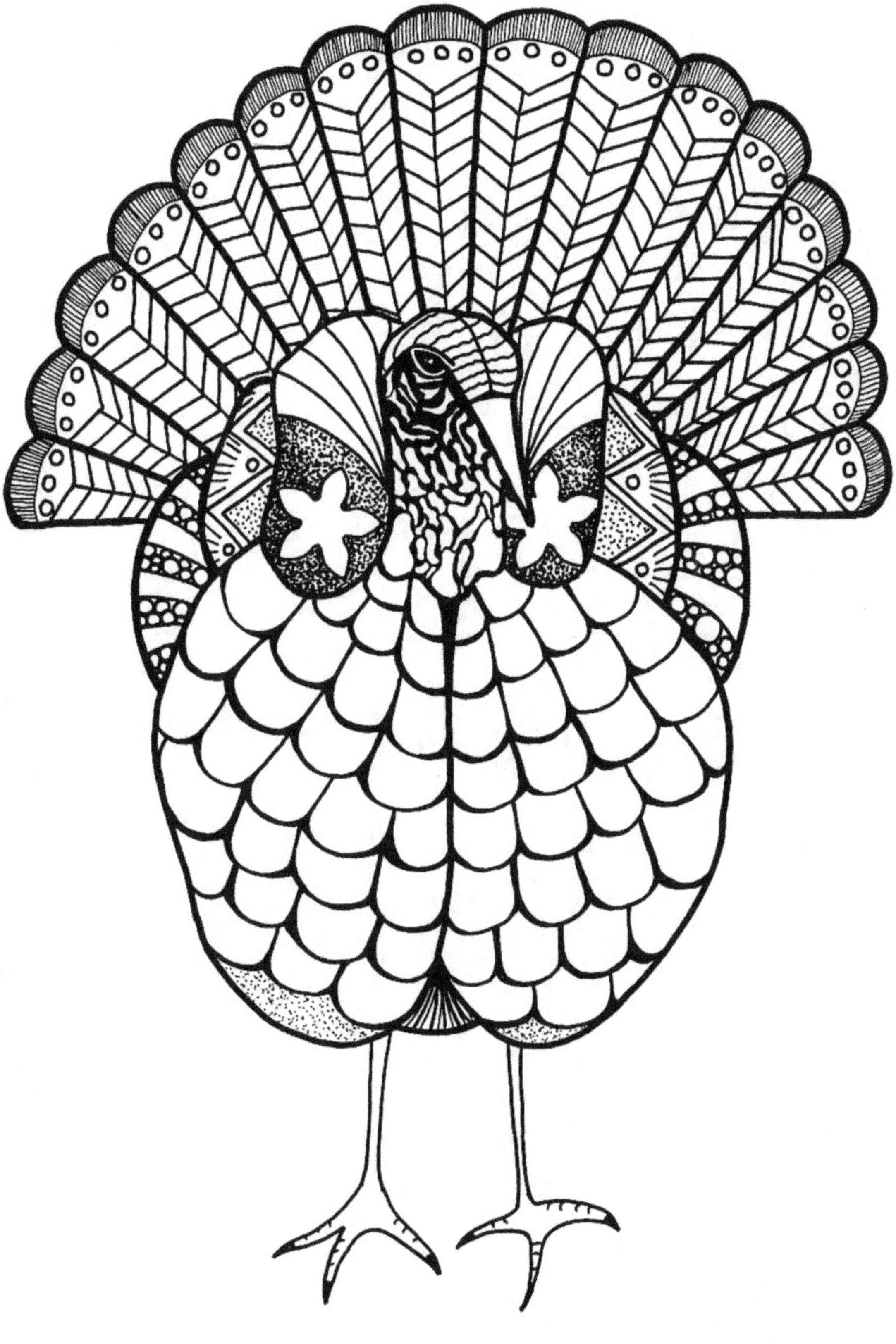

Enjoying this Notebook?

Please leave *Black Rose Press House* a review because we would love to know your thought, feedback, and opinions to create better products for you.

Please share how you creatively use your notebooks and journals.

THANKS

FOR YOUR SUPPORT

Scan This Qr Code And Visit Our Author Page At-

amazon.com

www.ingramcontent.com/pod-product-compliance
Lightning Source LLC
Chambersburg PA
CBHW081444220526
45466CB00008B/2505
9798558327700